How to Recognize Cults:

A Guide to Protecting Yourself from Manipulation and Control

Dirk Werner

HOW TO RECOGNIZE CULTS: A GUIDE TO PROTECTING YOURSELF FROM MANIPULATION AND CONTROL

First edition. November 16, 2024.

ISBN: 979-8230572978

Written by Dirk Werner.

Table of Contents

To all those who have found the strength to reclaim their lives from the grip of manipulation and control.

And to the families, friends, and communities who stand by them with unwavering support, offering light in the darkest of times.

May this book serve as a guide, a shield, and a reminder that knowledge is power, and that no one is truly alone.

Power corrupts, and absolute power corrupts absolutely.

Lord Acton

1 Understanding Cults

1.1 Definition and Characteristics

Understanding cults begins with a clear definition, which is essential for recognizing their presence in society today. A cult can be described as a social group that exhibits intense devotion to a particular leader, ideology, or set of beliefs, often at the expense of individual autonomy and critical thinking. This definition encompasses various types of cults, including religious sects, political movements, and self-help organizations that manipulate members through psychological control.

Cults typically share several defining characteristics that distinguish them from mainstream groups. One prominent feature is the presence of an authoritarian leadership structure where leaders demand absolute loyalty and obedience from followers. This dynamic fosters an environment where dissent is not tolerated, creating a culture of fear and dependency among members.

Another characteristic is the use of manipulative psychological techniques to maintain control over members. The BITE Model—Behavior, Information, Thought, Emotion—serves as a framework for understanding how cults exert influence. For instance, behavior control may involve regulating daily activities or enforcing strict codes of conduct. Information control restricts access to outside viewpoints or critical information about the group itself. Thought control shapes members' beliefs through indoctrination practices that discourage independent thinking. Lastly, emotional control manipulates feelings to create guilt or fear regarding leaving the group.

The vulnerability of individuals to cult recruitment varies based on personal circumstances such as emotional distress or social isolation. Those seeking community or purpose may find themselves drawn into these groups under the guise of support and belonging. Real-life stories illustrate how seemingly ordinary people can become ensnared in cult dynamics due to these vulnerabilities.

Recognizing warning signs is crucial for prevention; red flags include charismatic leaders who claim exclusive knowledge or truth and environments that promote isolation from family and friends. By understanding these definitions and characteristics, individuals can better identify potential cult influences in their lives or those around them.

1.2 Types of Cults

Understanding the various types of cults is crucial for recognizing their distinct characteristics and the specific ways they operate within society. Cults can be broadly categorized into several types, each with unique features that influence their recruitment strategies, belief systems, and methods of control. This classification not only aids in identifying these groups but also helps in understanding the psychological and social dynamics at play.

One prominent type is **religious cults**, which often center around a charismatic leader who claims to possess divine insight or special knowledge. These groups typically promote a worldview that diverges significantly from mainstream religious beliefs, often employing apocalyptic narratives to instill fear and urgency among followers. Examples include the Branch Davidians and Heaven's Gate, both of which attracted attention due to their extreme beliefs and tragic outcomes.

Political cults represent another category, where ideology supersedes individual autonomy. These groups may advocate for radical political change or revolutionary ideologies, often using manipulation tactics to maintain loyalty among members. The People's Temple led by Jim Jones serves as a historical example; it began as a progressive movement but devolved into a tragic mass suicide under authoritarian control.

Self-help cults, on the other hand, focus on personal development and empowerment but can quickly shift towards exploitative practices. These organizations often promise transformation through exclusive teachings or methodologies while isolating members from outside influences. Landmark Education is an example where participants are encouraged to undergo intense emotional experiences that reinforce group loyalty.

Additionally, there are **commercial cults**, which prioritize profit over genuine belief systems. These groups may use deceptive marketing practices to recruit individuals into multi-level marketing schemes disguised as community-building efforts. Such organizations can create dependency through financial pressure and social isolation from non-members.

The categorization of cults highlights the diverse motivations behind their formation and operation. By recognizing these types, individuals can better understand how different cult dynamics manifest in real-world scenarios, ultimately fostering greater awareness and prevention strategies against potential exploitation.

1.3 Distinguishing Cults from Other Groups

Distinguishing cults from other social or religious groups is essential for understanding their unique characteristics and the potential risks they pose to individuals and society. While many organizations may exhibit some traits associated with cults, not all fit the definition. This section explores key factors that help differentiate cults from benign groups, emphasizing aspects such as leadership structure, belief systems, and member dynamics.

One of the most significant distinguishing features of cults is their authoritarian leadership style. Cult leaders often possess a charismatic presence and claim exclusive access to truth or divine insight. This contrasts sharply with more traditional organizations where leadership is typically more democratic or accountable. For instance, in mainstream religions like Christianity or Buddhism, leaders are often subject to community oversight and can be challenged by congregants. In contrast, cult leaders maintain absolute control over their followers' beliefs and actions, creating an environment where dissent is not tolerated.

The belief systems within cults also tend to diverge markedly from those of conventional groups. Cults frequently promote ideologies that are apocalyptic or radically transformative, instilling a sense of urgency among members to adhere strictly to the group's teachings. This can lead to isolation from outside influences, as seen in groups like the Heaven's Gate movement, which believed in transcending earthly existence through extreme measures. In contrast, mainstream organizations generally encourage critical thinking and engagement with broader societal values.

Another critical aspect is the psychological manipulation employed by cults to maintain loyalty among members. Techniques such as love bombing—where new recruits are showered with affection—and fear tactics—such as threats of spiritual consequences for leaving—are common in cult environments. These methods create dependency on the group for emotional support and validation, making it difficult for individuals to leave even when they recognize harmful practices. Conversely, healthy organizations foster autonomy and personal growth without coercive tactics.

In summary, while various groups may share superficial similarities with cults—such as strong community bonds or unique beliefs—their fundamental differences lie in leadership dynamics, belief structures, and member treatment. Recognizing these distinctions is crucial for identifying potentially harmful environments and protecting vulnerable individuals from exploitation.

2 Historical Context of Cults

2.1 Notable Cults in History

The study of notable cults throughout history provides critical insights into the social, psychological, and cultural dynamics that enable such groups to thrive. Understanding these historical examples is essential for recognizing patterns that persist in contemporary society. Cults often emerge during periods of social upheaval or change, exploiting vulnerabilities within individuals and communities.

- One of the most infamous cults in history is the Peoples Temple, led by Jim Jones. Established in the 1950s, this group initially promoted racial equality and social justice but ultimately devolved into a tragic mass suicide in Jonestown, Guyana, in 1978.

- The event claimed over 900 lives and highlighted how charismatic leadership can manipulate followers into extreme actions under the guise of utopian ideals.

Another significant example is Heaven's Gate, founded by Marshall Applewhite and Bonnie Nettles in the 1970s. This group combined elements of Christianity with science fiction beliefs about extraterrestrial life. In 1997, 39 members committed suicide in California, believing they would ascend to a spaceship following the Hale-Bopp comet. This incident underscores how apocalyptic ideologies can lead individuals to drastic measures when intertwined with deep-seated fears and hopes.

The Branch Davidians are also noteworthy; their standoff with federal agents at Waco, Texas, in 1993 ended tragically with a fire that killed many members. Led by David Koresh, this group exemplified how religious fervor can escalate into violent confrontations when authority challenges deeply held beliefs.

These historical cases reveal common themes: authoritarian leadership styles, isolation from outside influences, and manipulation through fear or hope. They serve as cautionary tales about the potential for ordinary individuals to become ensnared in destructive belief systems. By studying these cults' rise and fall, we gain valuable lessons on human psychology and societal vulnerabilities that remain relevant today.

2.2 Social Factors Contributing to Cult Formation

The formation of cults is often deeply intertwined with various social factors that create fertile ground for their emergence. Understanding these factors is crucial, as they reveal how societal dynamics can lead individuals to seek belonging and meaning in unconventional groups. Cults frequently arise in contexts marked by social dislocation, economic instability, or cultural shifts, where traditional structures fail to provide adequate support.

One significant social factor is the sense of alienation experienced by individuals in modern society. As communities become more fragmented due to urbanization and technological advancements, many people find themselves isolated and disconnected from meaningful relationships. This loneliness can drive individuals to seek out groups that promise a sense of belonging and community, often leading them into the arms of cults that exploit these vulnerabilities.

Additionally, periods of crisis—whether economic downturns, political upheaval, or natural disasters—can catalyze cult formation. During such times, individuals may feel a loss of control over their lives and seek solace in charismatic leaders who offer clear answers and a sense of purpose. For instance, the rise of the Peoples Temple during the civil rights movement capitalized on widespread discontent with societal injustices, drawing followers who were eager for change but found themselves ensnared in a destructive ideology.

The role of social networks cannot be overlooked either; personal connections often facilitate entry into cults. Friends or family members who are already involved can act as conduits for recruitment, making it easier for newcomers to accept radical beliefs without critical scrutiny. This phenomenon highlights how peer pressure and the desire for acceptance can override individual skepticism.

Moreover, cultural narratives play a pivotal role in shaping perceptions about spirituality and authority. In societies where traditional religious institutions are losing influence, alternative belief systems gain traction. The blending of popular culture with spiritual ideologies—such as those seen in Heaven's Gate—demonstrates how contemporary myths can resonate with existential fears and aspirations.

In summary, understanding the social factors contributing to cult formation reveals not only the vulnerabilities within individuals but also broader societal trends that enable such groups to thrive. By examining these dynamics closely, we gain insights into preventing future occurrences while fostering healthier community connections.

2.3 Psychological Factors Influencing Membership

The psychological landscape of individuals plays a crucial role in their susceptibility to cult membership. Understanding these factors is essential for comprehending why certain individuals are drawn to such groups, often at the expense of their well-being and autonomy. Cults frequently exploit psychological vulnerabilities, offering solutions to existential dilemmas that resonate deeply with potential members.

One significant psychological factor is the search for identity and purpose. In an increasingly complex world, many individuals grapple with questions about their place in society and the meaning of life. Cults often present themselves as providing clear answers and a strong sense of belonging, which can be particularly appealing to those feeling lost or disillusioned. For instance, during times of personal crisis —such as loss, trauma, or major life transitions—individuals may become more receptive to radical ideologies that promise transformation and clarity.

Another critical aspect is cognitive dissonance, a psychological phenomenon where individuals experience discomfort from holding conflicting beliefs or values. Cults adeptly manipulate this dissonance by gradually introducing new beliefs while simultaneously reinforcing loyalty through social pressure and emotional manipulation. This process can lead members to rationalize their involvement despite any initial reservations they may have had about the group's practices or doctrines.

The role of charismatic leadership cannot be overstated; leaders often possess traits that evoke admiration and trust among followers. These leaders typically employ techniques such as love bombing—showering new recruits with affection and attention—to create an emotional bond that makes it difficult for individuals to leave once they are entrenched in the group. The psychological impact of such tactics can lead to dependency on the leader for validation and direction.

Moreover, cults frequently utilize isolation strategies that sever ties with outside influences, further entrenching members within the group's ideology. This isolation not only reinforces loyalty but also diminishes critical thinking by limiting exposure to alternative viewpoints. As members become more isolated from friends and family who might challenge their beliefs, they find themselves increasingly reliant on the cult for social support and affirmation.

In summary, understanding the psychological factors influencing cult membership reveals how deeply rooted human needs—such as belongingness, identity formation, and emotional security—can be exploited by manipulative groups. By recognizing these dynamics, we can better equip individuals with tools for resilience against such coercive environments.

3 The BITE Model of Control

3.1 Behavior Control

Behavior control is a fundamental aspect of the BITE Model, serving as a primary mechanism through which cults manipulate and dominate their members. This form of control encompasses various strategies aimed at regulating the actions and interactions of individuals within the group, ultimately fostering dependency on the cult's leadership and ideology.

One prevalent technique employed in behavior control is **isolation.** Cults often encourage or enforce physical separation from family, friends, and society at large. This isolation not only limits external influences but also creates an environment where members are more susceptible to indoctrination. For instance, many cults establish communal living arrangements that reinforce group cohesion while simultaneously severing ties with the outside world.

Monitoring is another critical element of behavior control. Members may be subjected to constant surveillance by leaders or fellow members, creating an atmosphere of fear and compliance. This can manifest in various forms, such as mandatory reporting on each other's activities or public confessions of perceived wrongdoings. Such practices instill a sense of guilt and shame that further binds individuals to the group.

Cults frequently employ **ritualistic practices** to regulate behavior as well. These rituals can range from daily meetings to elaborate ceremonies that reinforce group identity and loyalty. By participating in these activities, members internalize the group's values and beliefs, making it increasingly difficult for them to question or leave the organization.

The use of **rewards and punishments** also plays a significant role in behavior control. Positive reinforcement for adherence to group norms —such as praise or privileges—contrasts sharply with punitive measures for dissent or non-compliance, which can include shunning or emotional manipulation. This dual approach effectively conditions members to conform to expected behaviors while discouraging any thoughts of rebellion.

Ultimately, understanding behavior control within cults is crucial for recognizing how these groups operate and exert influence over their members' lives. By identifying these tactics—such as isolation, monitoring, ritualistic practices, and reward systems—individuals can better protect themselves from falling prey to manipulative organizations.

3.2 Information Control

Information control is a pivotal component of the BITE Model, serving as a mechanism through which cults manipulate the perceptions and beliefs of their members. By controlling access to information, these groups can shape narratives, suppress dissenting viewpoints, and create an environment where only the cult's ideology is accepted as truth. This manipulation not only reinforces loyalty but also fosters a sense of dependency on the group for knowledge and understanding.

One primary method of information control is **restricting access to external sources.** Cults often discourage or outright prohibit members from engaging with outside media, literature, or even conversations that could introduce alternative perspectives. For instance, many groups will label external information as "toxic" or "dangerous," creating an atmosphere where curiosity about the outside world is viewed as a betrayal. This isolation from diverse viewpoints ensures that members remain within a bubble of indoctrination.

Reinterpretation of facts is another tactic employed by cults to maintain control over information. Leaders may present distorted versions of events or teachings that align with the group's narrative while dismissing any contradictory evidence. This selective presentation can lead members to internalize false beliefs about themselves and their place in the world. For example, historical events may be reframed to glorify the cult's origins or justify its practices, further entrenching members in their worldview.

Cults also utilize **emotional manipulation** regarding information dissemination. Members are often subjected to intense emotional experiences during meetings or rituals that reinforce specific messages while discrediting opposing views. These emotionally charged environments make it difficult for individuals to critically assess what they are being told; instead, they may accept these messages uncritically due to fear of social ostracism or guilt associated with questioning authority.

The use of **confidentiality agreements** can further entrench information control within cults. Members may be required to keep certain teachings or practices secret from outsiders and even from each other, fostering an atmosphere of mistrust and paranoia. This secrecy not only isolates individuals but also creates barriers against seeking help or validation from those outside the group.

In summary, understanding how information control operates within cults reveals critical insights into their manipulative strategies. By recognizing tactics such as restricting access to external sources, reinterpretation of facts, emotional manipulation, and confidentiality agreements, individuals can better equip themselves against such coercive influences.

3.3 Thought and Emotion Control

Thought and emotion control is a critical aspect of the BITE Model, serving as a mechanism through which cults manipulate the internal landscapes of their members. By influencing how individuals think and feel, these groups can create an environment where dissent is minimized, loyalty is maximized, and personal autonomy is significantly diminished. This manipulation often leads to profound psychological changes that align members' beliefs and emotions with the group's ideology.

One prevalent method of thought control involves **cognitive dissonance**, where members are encouraged to adopt beliefs or behaviors that conflict with their previous values. This dissonance creates discomfort, prompting individuals to rationalize or justify their new beliefs in order to alleviate the psychological tension. For example, a member who previously valued independence may be taught that true freedom comes from complete submission to the group's authority. Over time, this reprogramming can lead to a complete overhaul of personal identity.

Emotional manipulation plays an equally significant role in maintaining control over members' thoughts and feelings. Cults often employ techniques such as love bombing—where new recruits are showered with affection and attention—to foster dependency on the group for emotional fulfillment. Once this bond is established, leaders may then introduce fear-based tactics, such as threats of social ostracism or spiritual condemnation for those who question or dissent. This cycle of affection followed by fear creates an emotional rollercoaster that keeps members engaged while suppressing critical thinking.

The use of **guilt and shame** further entrenches thought control within cult environments. Members are frequently reminded of their perceived shortcomings or failures in adhering to group norms, leading them to internalize negative self-perceptions. This emotional burden makes it difficult for individuals to challenge the status quo; instead, they may feel compelled to work harder to prove their worthiness within the group's hierarchy.

In summary, understanding thought and emotion control reveals how deeply cults can influence individual psychology. By employing strategies like cognitive dissonance, emotional manipulation through love bombing and fear tactics, as well as guilt-inducing practices, these groups effectively reshape not only what members believe but also how they feel about themselves and their place within the world.

3.4 Modern Digital Cults: How Technology Amplifies Manipulation

Introduction: The Rise of Online Influence

The digital age has transformed the landscape of cults and manipulation. Where once cults relied on physical gatherings and face-to-face recruitment, today's groups can reach millions of individuals with a few clicks. The internet, social media, and messaging platforms have created new pathways for cult leaders to spread their ideologies, recruit followers, and maintain control, often without ever meeting their members in person. This transformation has made cults more accessible—and more dangerous—than ever before.

In this section, we will explore how modern digital cults operate, using real-world examples to illustrate the ways in which technology has amplified traditional cult tactics. From political movements to spiritual influencers, financial scams to extremist groups, digital platforms have become the new battleground for manipulation and control.

Love Has Won – Spiritual Cults Online

Love Has Won demonstrates how spiritual cults use the internet to draw in followers. Through platforms like YouTube, the group spread Amy Carlson's teachings, attracting vulnerable individuals seeking spiritual guidance. Carlson, who claimed to be the reincarnation of various religious figures, led her followers to believe she had special divine knowledge that could heal the world.

Once followers were integrated into the community, they were subjected to emotional manipulation and isolation. Carlson, known as "Mother God," demanded absolute loyalty, isolating her followers from family and friends and requiring them to cut ties with the outside world. Her teachings combined New Age spirituality with apocalyptic warnings, creating a sense of urgency and fear that kept followers dependent on her guidance.

Love Has Won is a potent example of how spiritual ideologies can be twisted into cult-like structures through the power of online platforms. The internet allowed the group to reach and manipulate followers globally, creating a tightly controlled environment where dissent was not tolerated, and Carlson's authority remained unchallenged.

NXIVM – Online Self-Help and Personal Development Cults

NXIVM blurred the lines between self-help and cultic manipulation, using both physical and digital tools to control its members. Keith Raniere, the group's leader, promised personal growth and empowerment through his programs, which were marketed as exclusive seminars for high achievers. However, behind the scenes, NXIVM operated as a highly manipulative cult, particularly through its secret subgroup, DOS, where women were coerced into sexual slavery and branded with Raniere's initials.

NXIVM's use of digital communication played a significant role in maintaining control. Raniere and his inner circle used online platforms to recruit new members, gather compromising materials (so-called "collateral") on them, and maintain a constant line of communication to enforce loyalty. This digital dimension allowed Raniere to extend his influence far beyond in-person meetings, making it easier to control members and ensure their compliance through psychological and emotional manipulation.

NXIVM's downfall came when former members exposed the group's inner workings, but its success in blending online and offline control tactics serves as a cautionary tale of how self-help movements can evolve into dangerous cults.

Cryptocurrency Scams and Financial Cults – Manipulation Through Economic Pressure

Financial exploitation has become a hallmark of many modern online cults, particularly those operating under the guise of cryptocurrency or multi-level marketing (MLM) schemes. These groups lure individuals with promises of financial independence, often using online forums and social media platforms to create an illusion of exclusivity. By exploiting the fear of missing out (FOMO), these cults foster a sense of urgency and dependency on the group, isolating members from traditional financial advice and placing them in precarious financial situations.

Cryptocurrency scams, in particular, have seen a rise in cult-like behaviors. These scams often present themselves as investment communities, where members are promised inside knowledge and life-changing profits. Once drawn in, participants are pressured to recruit others or invest more money, often with little to no transparency about how the system works. Like traditional cults, these groups create a strong sense of belonging, where questioning the group's motives or results is seen as betrayal.

These financial cults prey on people's hopes and fears, using online platforms to reach wide audiences and create a sense of community around wealth-building schemes that are often fraudulent or unsustainable.

Flat Earth Movement – Pseudoscience in the Digital Age

The Flat Earth Movement is a striking example of how pseudoscientific beliefs can spread through digital platforms. Through YouTube and Facebook, followers of this movement reinforce their beliefs within echo chambers, where alternative views are dismissed, and mainstream science is distrusted. This isolation from reality mirrors the psychological control mechanisms found in traditional cults, where members are discouraged from questioning the group's core beliefs.

Flat Earthers often see themselves as part of an enlightened minority, believing that they have uncovered hidden truths about the world that most people are blind to. This sense of superiority, combined with the constant reinforcement of their beliefs through online communities, creates a powerful emotional bond between members and the movement. Like other digital cults, the Flat Earth Movement thrives on misinformation and the isolation of its members from opposing viewpoints.

Instagram Influencers and Digital Gurus – The Rise of Cult-like Spiritual Communities

Influencers on platforms like Instagram have increasingly adopted cult-like tactics to build spiritual or self-help communities online. These influencers often exploit their followers' emotional vulnerabilities, offering exclusive "spiritual knowledge" or life-transforming experiences in exchange for loyalty and financial contributions. The dynamics within these online communities can closely mirror those of traditional cults, with the influencer playing the role of a charismatic leader who demands absolute devotion.

Through emotionally charged posts, personal stories of transformation, and promises of enlightenment, influencers create a sense of urgency and exclusivity, drawing followers into a cycle of dependency. Followers are often encouraged to cut ties with negative influences in their lives—meaning anyone who questions the influencer's authority—and to invest more in the community, both emotionally and financially.

These digital gurus capitalize on the power of social media to amass large followings, often blurring the line between personal empowerment and manipulation.

Conclusion: The Future of Cults in the Digital Age

As the digital landscape continues to evolve, so too will the methods used by cults to recruit, manipulate, and control their members. The rise of online platforms has given cults unprecedented access to potential followers, allowing them to operate in secrecy and scale their influence globally. To resist these manipulative tactics, it is essential for individuals to develop digital literacy and critical thinking skills. While the platforms may change, the psychological control mechanisms remain the same.

4 Techniques of Influence

4.1 Love Bombing and Its Effects

Love bombing is a manipulative technique often employed by cults and high-control groups to attract and retain members. This strategy involves overwhelming an individual with affection, attention, and validation, creating an emotional bond that can be difficult to break. Understanding love bombing is crucial for recognizing the early signs of manipulation and coercion within such environments.

The initial phase of love bombing typically manifests as intense flattery, gifts, and constant communication. New recruits may feel special or chosen, leading them to lower their defenses. This barrage of positive reinforcement serves to create a dependency on the group for emotional support and validation. Over time, this dependency can evolve into a form of psychological control where individuals begin to prioritize the group's needs over their own.

One significant effect of love bombing is its ability to distort personal boundaries. Individuals who are subjected to this tactic may find themselves increasingly isolated from friends and family outside the group. The emotional high experienced during this phase can lead to cognitive dissonance when faced with any negative aspects of the group later on. Members might rationalize harmful behaviors or doctrines because they have been conditioned to associate love and acceptance solely with their involvement in the cult.

Moreover, love bombing can have long-lasting psychological effects even after leaving a cult. Survivors often struggle with feelings of worthlessness or abandonment once the initial affection fades away—this phenomenon is sometimes referred to as "post-cult syndrome." They may experience difficulty in forming healthy relationships due to mistrust or fear of being manipulated again.

Recognizing love bombing as a red flag is essential for prevention against cult influence. Awareness allows individuals to maintain critical thinking skills when approached by seemingly benevolent groups that offer unconditional support but may harbor ulterior motives. By understanding these dynamics, potential recruits can better protect themselves from falling into manipulative traps designed to exploit their vulnerabilities.

4.2 Isolation as a Manipulation Tool

Isolation serves as a powerful manipulation tool, particularly within high-control groups and cults. By severing an individual's connections to the outside world, manipulators can exert greater influence over their thoughts, beliefs, and behaviors. This tactic is often employed in conjunction with other manipulative strategies, such as love bombing, to create an environment where the individual feels increasingly dependent on the group for emotional support and validation.

The process of isolation typically begins subtly. Initially, members may be encouraged to spend more time with the group while gradually distancing themselves from friends and family. This can manifest through social pressure or guilt-tripping tactics that frame external relationships as detrimental or harmful. Over time, individuals may find themselves cut off from their previous support systems, leading to a heightened sense of vulnerability.

One significant aspect of isolation is its psychological impact. When individuals are removed from familiar environments and supportive relationships, they often experience feelings of loneliness and confusion. This emotional state makes them more susceptible to indoctrination since they begin to rely solely on the group's narrative for understanding their reality. The absence of external perspectives can lead to cognitive dissonance when confronted with contradictory information about the group's practices or beliefs.

Moreover, isolation fosters an environment where dissenting opinions are silenced or discouraged. Members may be conditioned to view any criticism of the group as a personal attack or betrayal. This creates a feedback loop where individuals become increasingly entrenched in their beliefs due to fear of ostracism or punishment for questioning authority figures within the group.

Real-world examples abound in various cults throughout history where isolation has been effectively utilized as a control mechanism. For instance, during the early stages of recruitment into groups like The People's Temple or

Heaven's Gate, new members were often isolated from their families under the guise of spiritual growth and enlightenment.

Recognizing isolation as a manipulation tool is crucial for both prevention and recovery from high-control environments. Awareness allows individuals to maintain critical thinking skills and seek out diverse perspectives that challenge narrow viewpoints imposed by manipulative groups.

4.3 Guilt and Doctrine-Based Control

The use of guilt as a mechanism for control is a pervasive tactic in high-control groups, particularly those that adhere to strict doctrines. This method exploits an individual's moral compass, creating an environment where members feel compelled to conform to the group's beliefs and practices out of fear of failing their perceived obligations. The interplay between guilt and doctrine not only reinforces loyalty but also stifles dissent, making it a powerful tool for manipulation.

At the core of this strategy lies the doctrine itself, which often includes rigid moral codes that dictate acceptable behavior. Members are frequently reminded of these standards through sermons, literature, or group discussions. When individuals fail to meet these expectations, they may experience intense feelings of guilt, which can be exacerbated by public shaming or private reprimands from leaders or peers. This emotional turmoil serves to reinforce compliance; members become increasingly reliant on the group for validation and forgiveness.

Moreover, guilt can be weaponized against those who question or challenge the group's teachings. Dissenters may be labeled as "sinners" or "unfaithful," leading them to internalize feelings of shame that discourage further questioning. This creates a culture where conformity is not just encouraged but enforced through emotional manipulation. The fear of being ostracized or condemned can lead individuals to suppress their doubts and fully embrace the doctrine, even if it conflicts with their personal values.

Real-world examples illustrate this dynamic vividly. In many religious cults, members are taught that straying from the doctrine equates to betrayal not only against the group but also against a higher power. Such teachings instill a profound sense of responsibility towards both the community and divine expectations, making it difficult for individuals to break free from these psychological chains.

Understanding how guilt operates within doctrine-based control mechanisms is crucial for recognizing manipulative environments. By fostering awareness around these tactics, individuals can develop resilience against such influences and maintain their autonomy in decision-making processes.

5 Recognizing Warning Signs

5.1 Red Flags in Leadership Dynamics

Recognizing red flags in leadership dynamics is crucial for identifying potentially harmful group environments, including cults. These warning signs often manifest through specific behaviors and patterns exhibited by leaders that can indicate a toxic or manipulative atmosphere. Understanding these dynamics not only aids individuals in protecting themselves but also empowers communities to foster healthier relationships within organizations.

One of the most significant red flags is the presence of authoritarian leadership. Leaders who demand absolute obedience and discourage dissent create an environment where critical thinking is stifled. This dynamic can lead to a culture of fear, where members feel compelled to conform to the leader's directives without question. For instance, historical examples like Jim Jones of Jonestown illustrate how charismatic leaders can manipulate followers into extreme loyalty, often at great personal cost.

Another alarming sign is the demand for unwavering loyalty from group members. When leaders insist on complete allegiance, it often serves as a mechanism to isolate individuals from outside influences and support systems. This isolation can be psychological as well as physical, leading members to cut ties with friends and family who may challenge the group's ideology or practices.

Control over information is also a critical indicator of unhealthy leadership dynamics. Leaders who restrict access to external sources of information or promote an echo chamber effect are effectively limiting members' ability to think independently. This tactic not only reinforces the leader's narrative but also cultivates dependency among followers, making them more susceptible to manipulation.

In conclusion, recognizing these red flags in leadership dynamics is essential for safeguarding against potential exploitation and manipulation within groups. By fostering awareness around these warning signs, individuals can better navigate their involvement in various organizations while promoting healthier interactions based on mutual respect and transparency.

- **Manipulation Tactics:** Techniques such as love bombing—where new recruits are showered with affection—can create an emotional bond that makes it difficult for individuals to leave.
- **Psycho-emotional Pressure:** The use of guilt and shame can further entrench members within the group, making them feel responsible for any perceived failures.
- **Lack of Transparency:** Leaders who avoid accountability or refuse to share decision-making processes often operate under a veil of secrecy that breeds mistrust and confusion among followers.

5.2 Indicators of Loyalty Demands

Understanding the indicators of loyalty demands is essential for recognizing environments that may foster unhealthy relationships and manipulation. Loyalty, when cultivated in a healthy manner, can enhance group cohesion and support. However, when it becomes a demand rather than a choice, it often signals deeper issues within the leadership dynamics of an organization or community.

A primary indicator of loyalty demands is the use of language that emphasizes exclusivity and belonging. Leaders may frequently employ phrases such as "us versus them," which creates an in-group mentality that pressures members to demonstrate unwavering allegiance to the group. This rhetoric not only fosters division but also instills a sense of obligation among followers to prioritize group interests over personal values or external relationships.

Another significant sign is the imposition of rituals or practices that reinforce loyalty. These can range from mandatory participation in group activities to public displays of commitment, such as pledges or oaths. Such practices serve dual purposes: they publicly affirm loyalty while simultaneously creating social pressure for compliance. Members who hesitate to participate may face ostracism or criticism, further entrenching their dependence on the group's approval.

The emotional manipulation associated with loyalty demands often manifests through guilt-tripping tactics. Leaders may exploit members' fears of abandonment or inadequacy by suggesting that any lack of commitment reflects poorly on their character or dedication to the cause. This psychological pressure can lead individuals to suppress doubts and concerns about the group's practices, reinforcing their isolation from outside perspectives.

- The presence of gatekeeping behaviors where leaders control access to information about alternative viewpoints can also indicate loyalty demands.

- Additionally, leaders might create scenarios where questioning decisions is framed as disloyalty, effectively silencing dissenting voices.

- Finally, rewards for demonstrating loyalty—such as recognition or advancement—can further entrench these demands by incentivizing conformity over critical engagement.

In conclusion, recognizing these indicators is vital for individuals navigating potentially manipulative environments. By understanding how loyalty can be demanded rather than freely given, members can better assess their involvement and seek healthier relational dynamics within groups.

5.3 Information Control Mechanisms

Information control mechanisms are critical tools employed by leaders and organizations to shape perceptions, manage narratives, and maintain authority over their members. These mechanisms can significantly influence the dynamics of loyalty and dissent within a group, often leading to environments where questioning or alternative viewpoints are systematically suppressed.

One prevalent method of information control is the selective dissemination of information. Leaders may choose to share only certain facts or perspectives that align with their agenda while withholding contradictory evidence. This creates an echo chamber effect, where members are exposed solely to ideas that reinforce existing beliefs, thereby limiting critical thinking and independent analysis. For instance, in high-control groups, members might receive curated updates that glorify leadership decisions while downplaying any negative consequences or dissenting opinions.

Another tactic involves the use of disinformation or misinformation strategies. By spreading false narratives or distorting facts about external entities—such as competitors or critics—leaders can manipulate how members perceive threats and allies alike. This not only fosters a sense of unity against perceived enemies but also discourages individuals from seeking out alternative sources of information that could challenge the group's narrative.

The establishment of gatekeeping roles further exemplifies information control mechanisms. In many organizations, certain individuals are designated as "gatekeepers" who filter what information reaches the broader group. This role can be particularly insidious; it allows leaders to maintain a façade of transparency while effectively controlling the flow of information. Members may feel compelled to rely on these gatekeepers for insights, inadvertently reinforcing their dependence on leadership for understanding key issues.

- Additionally, creating an environment where questioning is equated with disloyalty serves as a powerful deterrent against dissent.

- Leaders may also employ surveillance tactics—monitoring communications and interactions—to ensure compliance with established narratives.

- Finally, rewards for adherence to controlled narratives can further entrench these mechanisms by incentivizing conformity over critical engagement.

In summary, recognizing these information control mechanisms is essential for individuals navigating potentially manipulative environments. By understanding how access to knowledge is restricted and shaped within groups, members can better assess their involvement and seek healthier relational dynamics that encourage open dialogue and diverse perspectives

6 Identifying Vulnerable Individuals

6.1 Psychological Traits at Risk for Influence

Understanding the psychological traits that render individuals susceptible to influence is crucial in recognizing and mitigating the risks associated with cults. Certain characteristics can predispose individuals to manipulation, making them more vulnerable to the coercive tactics employed by these groups.

One significant trait is low self-esteem, which often leads individuals to seek external validation and belonging. Cults exploit this need by offering a sense of community and acceptance, creating an environment where members feel valued and important. This dynamic can be particularly appealing to those who have experienced social isolation or rejection in their lives.

Another critical factor is a high level of suggestibility. Individuals who are more open to new ideas or experiences may find themselves easily swayed by persuasive leaders or compelling narratives presented by cults. This trait can be exacerbated by emotional distress or life transitions, such as loss or trauma, during which people are more likely to seek solace in alternative belief systems.

Cognitive rigidity also plays a role; those who struggle with flexible thinking may find it challenging to question the doctrines imposed by cults. This inflexibility can lead to groupthink, where dissenting opinions are suppressed in favor of conformity, further entrenching members within the organization's ideology.

Additionally, individuals with a strong desire for certainty may gravitate towards cults that provide clear answers and structured beliefs. The allure of absolute truths offered by these groups can be particularly enticing for those grappling with uncertainty in their lives.

Lastly, emotional dependency is a significant risk factor. Individuals who rely heavily on others for emotional support may become enmeshed in cult dynamics that foster dependency on the group for validation and identity. This reliance can make it exceedingly difficult for them to extricate themselves from harmful situations once they become entrenched.

Recognizing these psychological traits not only aids in identifying vulnerable individuals but also emphasizes the importance of fostering resilience through education and critical thinking skills. By understanding these vulnerabilities, society can better equip individuals against manipulative influences and promote healthier interpersonal relationships.

6.2 Life Circumstances That Increase Vulnerability

Life circumstances play a pivotal role in shaping an individual's vulnerability to manipulation and coercion, particularly by groups such as cults. Understanding these circumstances is essential for identifying at-risk individuals and developing strategies to protect them from exploitative influences.

One significant life circumstance that heightens vulnerability is experiencing major life transitions, such as divorce, job loss, or the death of a loved one. These events can create emotional turmoil and a sense of instability, prompting individuals to seek solace or belonging in new communities. Cults often capitalize on this need for support by presenting themselves as safe havens where members can find understanding and acceptance during difficult times.

Another critical factor is social isolation. Individuals who lack strong social networks or supportive relationships are more susceptible to the allure of cults that promise companionship and community. This isolation may stem from various sources, including geographic relocation, mental health issues, or previous negative experiences with social groups. The absence of a robust support system makes it easier for manipulative organizations to fill the void left by these connections.

Poverty and economic hardship also significantly contribute to vulnerability. Financial stress can lead individuals to make desperate choices in search of stability or security. Cults may offer financial assistance or employment opportunities that appear attractive but ultimately serve as tools for control and exploitation. The promise of financial relief can blind individuals to the underlying manipulative tactics employed by these groups.

Additionally, cultural factors such as immigration status can increase susceptibility. Immigrants may face unique challenges related to language barriers, discrimination, and unfamiliarity with local customs, making them more reliant on community support systems that could be predatory in nature.

Cults often target these populations by offering a sense of belonging while simultaneously exploiting their vulnerabilities.

In summary, recognizing how specific life circumstances—such as major transitions, social isolation, economic hardship, and cultural factors—contribute to individual vulnerability is crucial for prevention efforts. By addressing these issues through education and community support initiatives, society can help mitigate the risks associated with manipulative influences.

6.3 The Role of Critical Thinking Skills

Critical thinking skills are essential in identifying and mitigating the vulnerabilities that individuals face, particularly in contexts where manipulation and coercion are prevalent. These skills enable individuals to analyze situations, evaluate information critically, and make informed decisions, which is crucial when navigating complex social dynamics often exploited by cults and other manipulative groups.

One of the primary functions of critical thinking is to foster skepticism towards persuasive messages. Individuals equipped with strong critical thinking abilities can discern between genuine support systems and those that may have ulterior motives. For instance, when faced with a group promising emotional or financial relief during a life crisis, a critical thinker would question the group's intentions, scrutinize their claims, and seek corroborating evidence before committing to involvement. This analytical approach serves as a protective barrier against exploitation.

Moreover, critical thinking encourages self-reflection and awareness of cognitive biases that may cloud judgment. Many individuals fall prey to manipulative organizations due to inherent biases such as confirmation bias or the bandwagon effect. By cultivating an understanding of these biases through critical thinking training, individuals can better recognize when their decision-making processes are being influenced by external pressures or misleading narratives.

Education plays a pivotal role in enhancing critical thinking skills across various demographics. Programs aimed at teaching these skills can be integrated into community outreach initiatives targeting vulnerable populations—such as immigrants or those experiencing significant life transitions—who may lack access to traditional educational resources. Workshops focusing on logical reasoning, argument analysis, and media literacy can empower participants to navigate social interactions more effectively and resist coercive influences.

In conclusion, fostering critical thinking skills is vital for equipping individuals with the tools necessary to identify potential threats from manipulative groups. By promoting education that emphasizes analytical reasoning and self-awareness, society can create resilient communities capable of resisting exploitation while supporting one another through challenging life circumstances.

7 Impact on Mental Health

7.1 PTSD and Trauma Responses

The psychological aftermath of cult involvement can lead to significant mental health challenges, particularly in the form of Post-Traumatic Stress Disorder (PTSD) and various trauma responses. Understanding these conditions is crucial for recognizing the profound impact that cult experiences can have on individuals, as well as for developing effective recovery strategies.

PTSD is characterized by symptoms such as intrusive memories, avoidance behaviors, negative changes in mood and cognition, and heightened arousal. For former cult members, these symptoms often stem from traumatic experiences within the group, including emotional abuse, manipulation, and isolation from loved ones. The intensity of these experiences can lead to a pervasive sense of fear and helplessness that persists long after leaving the cult environment.

Trauma responses may vary widely among individuals based on their personal histories and the specific nature of their cult involvement. Some may exhibit hyper-vigilance or anxiety disorders due to constant surveillance or threats within the group. Others might experience dissociation as a coping mechanism during traumatic events, leading to difficulties in processing their experiences post-cult. This disconnection from reality can complicate recovery efforts by making it challenging for survivors to confront their pasts.

Moreover, identity loss is a common issue faced by ex-cult members. Many individuals enter cults seeking belonging or purpose but emerge feeling fragmented or unsure of who they are outside the group's ideology. This identity crisis can exacerbate feelings of depression and anxiety, further entrenching PTSD symptoms.

Effective treatment for PTSD in this context often requires specialized therapeutic approaches that address both trauma recovery and identity reconstruction. Techniques such as Eye Movement Desensitization and Reprocessing (EMDR) have shown promise in helping survivors process traumatic memories while cognitive-behavioral therapy (CBT) can assist in reshaping distorted beliefs about self-worth instilled during cult membership.

In conclusion, recognizing PTSD and trauma responses among former cult members is essential for providing appropriate support systems that facilitate healing. By understanding these psychological impacts, mental health professionals can better tailor interventions that promote resilience and reintegration into society.

7.2 Identity Loss Among Members

The phenomenon of identity loss among former cult members is a profound and often distressing aspect of their psychological recovery. Cults frequently employ manipulative techniques that strip individuals of their personal identities, replacing them with a collective identity dictated by the group's ideology. This transformation can lead to significant challenges in reintegrating into society after leaving the cult, as many individuals grapple with feelings of confusion and disconnection from their sense of self.

When individuals join a cult, they often do so in search of belonging or purpose, which can be particularly appealing during vulnerable periods in their lives. However, once immersed in the group, they may find that their personal beliefs, values, and even memories are systematically undermined. The process of indoctrination typically involves intense emotional manipulation and social isolation, which can result in a fragmented sense of self. As members become more entrenched within the cult's framework, they may lose touch with who they were before joining.

This identity crisis is exacerbated upon exiting the cult. Many former members report feeling like strangers to themselves; they struggle to reconcile their past experiences with their current realities. This dissonance can manifest as depression, anxiety, or even existential crises as individuals attempt to rediscover their identities outside the confines of the group's teachings. The absence of a supportive community further complicates this process; without the validation and acceptance previously found within the cult, many feel lost and isolated.

Rebuilding one's identity post-cult requires intentional effort and often professional support. Therapeutic approaches such as narrative therapy can be beneficial in helping survivors articulate their experiences and reconstruct a coherent life story that honors both their past within the cult and their aspirations for the future. Additionally, peer support groups provide essential spaces for sharing experiences and fostering connections that facilitate healing.

Ultimately, addressing identity loss is crucial for effective recovery from cult involvement. By recognizing this challenge as an integral part of healing, mental health professionals can better assist former members in reclaiming their identities and reintegrating into society with renewed strength and purpose.

7.3 Groupthink Phenomena in Cults

The concept of groupthink is particularly relevant in the context of cults, where the desire for harmony and conformity within a group can lead to irrational decision-making and a suppression of dissenting viewpoints. This psychological phenomenon occurs when members prioritize consensus over critical analysis, often resulting in poor choices that align with the group's ideology rather than reality. Understanding groupthink in cults is essential for comprehending how these organizations maintain control over their members and perpetuate harmful beliefs.

Cults often create an environment that fosters groupthink through various mechanisms, including isolation from outside influences, intense loyalty demands, and charismatic leadership. Members are frequently encouraged to view the world in binary terms—good versus evil—where questioning the group's beliefs is equated with betrayal. This black-and-white thinking not only stifles individual thought but also reinforces a collective identity that prioritizes group cohesion above all else.

One notable example of groupthink can be observed in high-profile cults such as Jonestown or Heaven's Gate, where leaders manipulated followers into making catastrophic decisions based on shared delusions. In these cases, dissent was not merely discouraged; it was actively punished, leading to tragic outcomes that could have been avoided had critical thinking been allowed to flourish. The pressure to conform can be so overwhelming that individuals may even suppress their own doubts or fears about the group's actions.

The consequences of groupthink extend beyond immediate decision-making failures; they can also contribute to long-term psychological damage among former members. After leaving a cult, individuals may struggle with trust issues and difficulty making independent decisions due to years spent suppressing their own thoughts and feelings. Therapeutic interventions aimed at addressing these issues often focus on rebuilding self-esteem and encouraging critical thinking skills as part of the recovery process.

In conclusion, understanding the dynamics of groupthink within cults provides valuable insights into how these organizations operate and maintain control over their members. By recognizing the signs of this phenomenon, mental health professionals can better support individuals seeking to reclaim their autonomy after exiting such groups.

8 Exiting a Cult

8.1 Stages of Leaving a Cult

Understanding the stages of leaving a cult is crucial for both individuals seeking to escape and those supporting them. The process is often complex, involving emotional, psychological, and social dimensions that can significantly impact recovery. Recognizing these stages helps in developing effective strategies for reintegration into society and rebuilding one's identity.

The first stage typically involves **awareness**. Members may begin to question the teachings or practices of the cult, often triggered by external influences such as conversations with friends or exposure to differing viewpoints. This cognitive dissonance can lead to feelings of confusion and fear, as members grapple with the implications of their doubts.

Following awareness is the stage of **contemplation**, where individuals weigh their options more seriously. They might start gathering information about life outside the cult, reflecting on personal experiences within it. This phase can be fraught with anxiety as members consider the potential consequences of leaving—loss of community, relationships, and identity.

The next stage is **decision-making**, where individuals commit to leaving. This decision often requires careful planning due to fears of retaliation from cult leaders or isolation from family and friends still within the group. Support networks become vital during this phase; trusted allies can provide encouragement and practical assistance in navigating exit strategies.

Once a member has left, they enter the **transition** stage. This period involves adjusting to life outside the cult's confines while dealing with residual feelings of guilt or shame associated with their past involvement. Many experience a profound sense of loss—not just for relationships but also for a previously held worldview that provided structure and meaning.

The final stage is **reintegration**, which focuses on rebuilding one's identity and establishing new connections in society. Counseling or support groups play an essential role here, helping former members process their experiences and develop healthy coping mechanisms. Successful reintegration fosters resilience against future manipulative influences while promoting personal growth.

8.2 Practical Steps for Exit Strategies

Developing effective exit strategies is essential for individuals seeking to leave a cult, as the process can be fraught with emotional and psychological challenges. A well-structured plan not only aids in the physical act of leaving but also supports mental resilience during the transition. This section outlines practical steps that can facilitate a smoother exit from a cult environment.

The first step involves **building a support network**. It is crucial for individuals to identify trusted friends, family members, or former cult members who can provide emotional and logistical support. Engaging with these allies before making any decisions allows individuals to share their feelings and concerns, which can help alleviate fears associated with leaving. Support groups specifically designed for ex-cult members can also offer valuable insights and encouragement.

Next, **gathering information** about life outside the cult is vital. Individuals should research various aspects of society they may have been isolated from, including social norms, job opportunities, and community resources. This knowledge helps reduce anxiety about the unknown and prepares them for reintegration into mainstream culture. Reading books or articles on personal experiences of others who have left similar groups can provide both inspiration and practical advice.

A critical component of an exit strategy is **developing a financial plan**. Many cults control their members' finances, so it's important to assess one's financial situation before leaving. Creating a budget that accounts for immediate needs—such as housing, food, and transportation—can ease the transition significantly. If possible, securing employment or saving money prior to departure will provide additional security during this vulnerable time.

Finally, **establishing boundaries** with remaining cult members is essential once an individual decides to leave. This may involve limiting contact with those still within the group or setting clear expectations regarding communication. Such boundaries help protect against manipulation or attempts at coercion from former peers or leaders who may try to dissuade them from their decision.

In conclusion, implementing these practical steps—building a support network, gathering information about life outside the cult, developing a financial plan, and establishing boundaries—can empower individuals in their journey toward freedom and self-discovery after leaving a cult.

8.3 Survivor Stories and Their Insights

Survivor stories serve as powerful narratives that illuminate the complex journey of individuals who have escaped cults. These personal accounts not only provide insight into the psychological and emotional toll of cult life but also offer invaluable lessons for those contemplating an exit. By sharing their experiences, survivors contribute to a broader understanding of the mechanisms of control employed by cults and the resilience required to reclaim one's identity.

One common theme in survivor stories is the profound sense of isolation experienced while within a cult. Many recount how they were cut off from family and friends, leading to a deep-seated fear of leaving due to potential ostracism. For instance, a former member might describe how their relationships with loved ones deteriorated over time, reinforcing their dependency on the group for social support. This highlights the importance of building connections with trusted individuals outside the cult before attempting an exit, as these relationships can provide crucial emotional backing during such a vulnerable transition.

Another significant insight from survivor narratives is the gradual realization of manipulation tactics used by cult leaders. Survivors often reflect on moments when they began questioning doctrines or practices that seemed contradictory or harmful. These epiphanies are pivotal; they mark the beginning of critical thinking that can lead to eventual departure. Sharing these realizations can empower others still trapped in similar situations, encouraging them to trust their instincts and seek clarity about their circumstances.

Moreover, many survivors emphasize the importance of post-cult therapy and support groups in facilitating healing after leaving a cult environment. They recount how professional counseling helped them process trauma and rebuild self-esteem shattered by years of indoctrination. Engaging with others who have shared similar experiences fosters a sense of community and belonging that is often lost during cult involvement.

In conclusion, survivor stories are not just tales of escape; they are rich sources of wisdom that underscore key aspects such as isolation, manipulation awareness, and the necessity for ongoing support post-exit. By amplifying these voices, we gain deeper insights into both individual resilience and collective recovery processes following life in a cult.

9 Recovery and Reintegration

9.1 Counseling Support Systems

The role of counseling support systems in the recovery and reintegration of individuals who have exited cults is paramount. These systems provide essential emotional, psychological, and social resources that facilitate healing from the trauma associated with cult involvement. Understanding the unique needs of former cult members is crucial for developing effective counseling strategies that address their specific experiences and challenges.

Counseling support systems often encompass a range of therapeutic approaches tailored to individual circumstances. Cognitive Behavioral Therapy (CBT) is particularly beneficial as it helps individuals reframe negative thought patterns instilled during their time in a cult. This method encourages critical thinking and empowers survivors to regain control over their beliefs and decisions, fostering a sense of autonomy that may have been stripped away.

Peer support groups also play a vital role in the recovery process. These groups create safe spaces where former members can share their experiences without fear of judgment. The shared understanding among participants fosters a sense of community, reducing feelings of isolation that many experience post-cult. Such environments not only validate individual experiences but also promote collective healing through shared narratives.

Moreover, integrating family therapy into counseling support systems can be transformative for both survivors and their loved ones. Cult involvement often strains familial relationships due to manipulation and secrecy; thus, addressing these dynamics is essential for rebuilding trust and communication within families. Family therapy sessions can help educate relatives about the psychological impacts of cults, equipping them with tools to support their loved ones effectively.

Finally, ongoing education about the nature of cults and their psychological effects is crucial for counselors themselves. Training programs focused on recognizing signs of manipulation and understanding the BITE Model can enhance therapists' ability to assist clients effectively. By staying informed about current trends in cult behavior—especially those utilizing digital platforms—counselors can better prepare themselves to guide survivors through their recovery journey.

9.2 Rebuilding Personal Identity Post-Cult

The journey of rebuilding personal identity after exiting a cult is a complex and deeply personal process. Individuals often find themselves grappling with a fragmented sense of self, as their identities were heavily influenced or even dictated by the cult's ideology. This reconstruction is not merely about reclaiming lost aspects of one's personality; it involves a profound re-evaluation of beliefs, values, and life goals that may have been suppressed during their time in the group.

One critical aspect of this rebuilding process is the need for self-exploration. Former members must engage in activities that allow them to rediscover their interests and passions outside the confines of cult doctrine. This can include pursuing hobbies, education, or new social connections that reflect their authentic selves rather than the identities imposed upon them by the cult. For instance, someone who was once discouraged from expressing creativity might take up painting or writing as a means to explore and express their individuality.

Additionally, establishing boundaries becomes essential in this phase. Many former cult members struggle with boundary issues due to years of manipulation and control. Learning to assert personal boundaries helps individuals regain autonomy over their lives and decisions. This can be facilitated through therapy or support groups where they can practice these skills in a safe environment, gradually building confidence in asserting their needs and desires.

Moreover, reconnecting with family and friends who may have been alienated during cult involvement plays a significant role in identity reconstruction. These relationships provide emotional support and validation as individuals navigate their new realities. Open communication about past experiences fosters understanding and healing within these relationships, allowing for mutual growth.

Finally, embracing uncertainty is an integral part of rebuilding identity post-cult. The transition from a rigid belief system to one that allows for ambiguity can be daunting but also liberating. Individuals are encouraged to explore various philosophies and worldviews without fear of judgment or repercussion—an opportunity to cultivate a more nuanced understanding of themselves and the world around them.

9.3 Navigating Relationships After Departure

Navigating relationships after leaving a cult is a critical aspect of the recovery and reintegration process. The departure from a high-control group often results in significant shifts in personal dynamics, as former members must reassess their connections with family, friends, and even new acquaintances. This transition can be both liberating and daunting, requiring careful consideration of how to rebuild trust and establish healthy boundaries.

One of the first challenges faced by individuals is reconnecting with family members who may have been alienated during their time in the cult. These relationships can be fraught with tension due to past grievances or misunderstandings stemming from the individual's previous beliefs. Open communication becomes essential; sharing experiences and feelings about the cult can foster empathy and understanding. For instance, a former member might express how their involvement affected their ability to maintain familial ties, which can help bridge gaps that were created during their absence.

Additionally, establishing new friendships poses its own set of challenges. Former cult members often find themselves navigating social situations where they must discern between genuine connections and those that may replicate past manipulative dynamics. Engaging in community activities or support groups specifically for ex-cult members can provide safe spaces to form new bonds based on shared experiences. These environments encourage mutual support while allowing individuals to practice vulnerability without fear of judgment.

Moreover, it is crucial for individuals to develop skills in setting boundaries within all types of relationships post-departure. Many former cult members struggle with boundary issues due to years of indoctrination that blurred personal limits. Learning to assertively communicate needs—whether it's saying no or expressing discomfort —can empower individuals as they navigate these new relational landscapes.

Finally, embracing change is vital when rebuilding relationships after leaving a cult. Individuals should remain open to evolving dynamics as they grow into their newfound identities outside the group's influence. This adaptability not only enhances personal growth but also enriches interactions with others who may be adjusting alongside them.

10 Case Studies of Historical Cults

10.1 Analysis of Jonestown

The tragic events at Jonestown in 1978 serve as a stark reminder of the potential dangers posed by cults and the psychological manipulation that can ensnare individuals. Founded by Jim Jones, the Peoples Temple initially attracted followers with its promises of social justice and community. However, as the group evolved, it became increasingly authoritarian, employing various psychological tactics to maintain control over its members.

One critical aspect of Jonestown's dynamics was the use of isolation. Members were physically removed from their previous lives and communities, which made them more susceptible to Jones's influence. This geographical separation not only cut off external support systems but also fostered an environment where dissent was discouraged. The BITE Model—Behavior, Information, Thought, Emotion—was evident in how Jones manipulated his followers' realities. For instance, he controlled information by limiting access to outside news and promoting a narrative that painted him as a savior figure.

Moreover, emotional manipulation played a significant role in maintaining loyalty among members. Techniques such as "love bombing" created an initial sense of belonging and acceptance that many found difficult to leave behind. As time progressed, however, this affection morphed into guilt and fear; members were often told they would face dire consequences for questioning Jones or considering leaving the group.

The culmination of these manipulative strategies led to the horrific mass suicide on November 18, 1978, where over 900 individuals lost their lives under coercive circumstances. This event highlights not only the extreme outcomes possible within cult environments but also underscores the importance of recognizing early warning signs associated with such groups.

In analyzing Jonestown, it becomes clear that understanding cult dynamics is essential for prevention efforts today. By studying historical cases like this one, we can better equip ourselves to identify manipulative behaviors and protect vulnerable individuals from similar fates in contemporary settings.

10.2 Examination of Heaven's Gate

The examination of Heaven's Gate provides critical insights into the psychological and social dynamics that can lead individuals to join and remain in a cult. Founded in the early 1970s by Marshall Applewhite and Bonnie Nettles, this group initially attracted followers with its unique blend of Christian eschatology and science fiction themes, particularly the belief in an impending apocalypse and the promise of ascension to a higher existence.

A significant aspect of Heaven's Gate was its emphasis on duality—members were taught to view themselves as both human beings and extraterrestrial souls trapped in physical bodies. This belief system created a profound sense of purpose among followers, who felt they were chosen for a special mission. The group's teachings included strict adherence to celibacy, communal living, and renunciation of worldly possessions, which fostered an environment where members could fully immerse themselves in their beliefs without external distractions.

Isolation played a crucial role in maintaining control over members. By encouraging followers to sever ties with family and friends outside the group, Applewhite effectively minimized dissenting opinions that could challenge their worldview. This tactic not only reinforced loyalty but also created an echo chamber where members' beliefs were continuously validated by one another. The BITE Model is evident here as well; behavior was controlled through rigorous schedules and practices, while information was tightly regulated through group teachings that emphasized their unique knowledge.

The culmination of these manipulative strategies led to the tragic mass suicide in March 1997, where 39 members took their lives believing they would ascend to a spacecraft following the Hale-Bopp comet. This event starkly illustrates how deeply ingrained beliefs can culminate in extreme actions when combined with psychological manipulation and isolation from societal norms.

In analyzing Heaven's Gate, it becomes clear that understanding such groups is essential for prevention efforts today. By studying their dynamics—particularly how they exploit existential fears—we can better equip ourselves to identify similar patterns in contemporary settings, ultimately protecting vulnerable individuals from falling prey to manipulative ideologies.

10.3 Lessons Learned from Past Events

The tragic events surrounding Heaven's Gate serve as a poignant reminder of the psychological and social mechanisms that can lead individuals into cult-like environments. Understanding these dynamics is crucial for both prevention and intervention strategies in contemporary society. One of the primary lessons learned is the importance of recognizing the signs of manipulation and control within groups, particularly those that exploit existential fears.

Isolation emerges as a key tactic used by cults to maintain control over their members. By severing ties with family and friends, groups like Heaven's Gate create an environment where dissenting opinions are minimized, fostering an echo chamber that reinforces their beliefs. This highlights the need for awareness among families and communities about the potential dangers posed by such isolation tactics. Open communication channels can serve as vital lifelines for individuals who may be vulnerable to recruitment by high-control groups.

Another significant lesson pertains to the role of charismatic leadership in cult dynamics. Leaders often possess a unique ability to articulate compelling narratives that resonate with followers' desires for belonging, purpose, or understanding of complex existential questions. This underscores the necessity for critical thinking skills and media literacy education, enabling individuals to discern manipulative rhetoric from genuine guidance.

- **Awareness of Psychological Manipulation:** Recognizing how emotional appeals can override rational thought is essential in preventing individuals from falling prey to cult ideologies.

- **Community Support Systems:** Establishing strong community networks can provide support for those questioning their involvement in high-control groups.

- **Cult Education Programs:** Implementing educational initiatives focused on identifying cult characteristics can empower individuals with knowledge to resist coercive influences.

The culmination of these insights emphasizes a proactive approach towards understanding and addressing the factors that contribute to cult formation and retention. By learning from past events like Heaven's Gate, society can better equip itself to protect vulnerable populations from similar fates, fostering resilience against manipulative ideologies while promoting healthy community engagement.

11 Modern-Day Cults

11.1 Online Recruitment Strategies

The rise of the internet has transformed the landscape of cult recruitment, making it easier for modern-day cults to reach potential members across vast distances. Understanding these online recruitment strategies is crucial for recognizing and countering their influence. Cults leverage digital platforms to create a sense of community and belonging, often targeting vulnerable individuals who may be seeking connection or purpose.

One prevalent strategy involves the use of social media platforms where cults can curate content that resonates with specific audiences. By employing algorithms that promote engagement, they can effectively reach individuals who express interest in related topics such as spirituality, self-improvement, or alternative lifestyles. This targeted approach allows cults to identify and exploit emotional vulnerabilities, drawing in those who are searching for answers or support.

Another tactic is the creation of engaging websites and forums that present an idealized version of life within the group. These sites often feature testimonials from current members highlighting personal transformations and communal experiences. Such narratives serve to normalize the group's beliefs while simultaneously isolating potential recruits from external perspectives that might challenge their views.

- **Webinars and Online Workshops:** Many cults host free webinars or workshops that promise personal growth or enlightenment. These events often serve as gateways for deeper involvement, gradually introducing participants to more extreme ideologies.

- **Influencer Partnerships:** Collaborating with social media influencers allows cults to tap into established follower bases, presenting their messages in a relatable manner that feels authentic and trustworthy.

- **Email Campaigns:** Cults frequently utilize email marketing strategies to maintain contact with interested individuals, providing them with curated content designed to reinforce group ideology over time.

The anonymity afforded by online interactions also plays a significant role in recruitment strategies. Individuals may feel emboldened to explore new ideas without immediate judgment from friends or family, allowing cults to foster deeper connections through private messaging or closed groups. As these tactics evolve alongside technology, it becomes increasingly important for society to remain vigilant against such manipulative practices.

11.2 Digital Manipulation Tactics

The digital age has ushered in a new era of manipulation tactics employed by modern-day cults, leveraging technology to exert influence and control over potential recruits. Understanding these tactics is essential for recognizing the subtle ways in which individuals can be drawn into harmful ideologies and communities. Cults utilize various digital platforms not only for recruitment but also for maintaining control over their members through psychological manipulation.

One significant tactic involves the use of persuasive messaging that exploits cognitive biases. Cults often craft messages that resonate with an individual's existing beliefs or desires, creating a false sense of validation and understanding. For instance, they may employ confirmation bias by presenting information that aligns with a recruit's worldview while dismissing contradictory evidence. This selective exposure reinforces loyalty and discourages critical thinking, making it difficult for individuals to question the group's teachings.

Additionally, cults frequently engage in emotional manipulation through targeted content designed to elicit strong feelings such as fear, guilt, or euphoria. By sharing emotionally charged testimonials or dramatic narratives about personal transformation, they create an environment where recruits feel compelled to conform to group norms. This emotional engagement is often amplified through multimedia content—videos, podcasts, and live streams—that fosters a sense of immediacy and connection.

The use of gamification is another innovative strategy employed by cults to enhance member engagement and commitment. By incorporating elements such as rewards systems or challenges within their online platforms, cults can create a compelling experience that encourages participation and investment in the group's ideology. This approach not only keeps members active but also fosters competition among them, further solidifying their allegiance to the community.

Moreover, the anonymity provided by online interactions allows cults to manipulate social dynamics effectively. Members may feel more comfortable sharing personal information or engaging in discussions without fear of judgment from outsiders. This creates an echo chamber effect where dissenting opinions are silenced, reinforcing conformity within the group while isolating individuals from external influences that could challenge their beliefs.

11.3 Echo Chambers in the Digital Age

The phenomenon of echo chambers has gained significant traction in the digital age, particularly within the context of modern-day cults. These online environments foster a sense of community among like-minded individuals while simultaneously isolating them from opposing viewpoints. This isolation is crucial for cults, as it reinforces their ideologies and diminishes critical thinking, making it easier to manipulate members.

One of the primary mechanisms through which echo chambers operate is algorithmic filtering on social media platforms. Algorithms are designed to curate content that aligns with users' previous interactions, creating a feedback loop that amplifies existing beliefs. For instance, if an individual engages with content promoting conspiracy theories or extremist ideologies, they are likely to be inundated with similar material. This not only solidifies their beliefs but also creates a distorted perception of reality where dissenting opinions are virtually non-existent.

Moreover, the anonymity afforded by online interactions allows individuals to express themselves without fear of judgment or reprisal. In these spaces, members often share personal stories and experiences that resonate deeply with one another, further entrenching their shared beliefs. The emotional bonds formed in these echo chambers can be incredibly powerful; they create a sense of belonging that is difficult to replicate outside the group. As members become more invested emotionally and socially, they may find it increasingly challenging to question or leave the group.

The role of influencers within these echo chambers cannot be understated. Charismatic leaders often emerge who serve as gatekeepers of information, dictating what is acceptable discourse within the group. Their authority can stifle dissent and promote conformity by framing any criticism as an attack on the community itself. This dynamic not only perpetuates loyalty but also cultivates an environment where questioning becomes synonymous with betrayal.

In conclusion, echo chambers in the digital age represent a formidable challenge for individuals seeking truth and understanding amidst a sea of misinformation and manipulation. By recognizing how these environments function—through algorithmic reinforcement, emotional bonding, and authoritative influence—individuals can better equip themselves to navigate complex ideological landscapes and resist coercive narratives propagated by modern-day cults.

12 Prevention Strategies

12.1 Educating Others About Dangers

Educating others about the dangers of cults is a crucial step in prevention strategies. Awareness can empower individuals to recognize manipulative behaviors and protect themselves and their loved ones from potential harm. By disseminating knowledge about the characteristics and tactics of cults, we can foster a more informed society that is less susceptible to such influences.

One effective method of education involves sharing real-life stories of individuals who have been affected by cults. These narratives not only humanize the issue but also illustrate the psychological manipulation involved. For instance, survivors often recount experiences of isolation, emotional abuse, and identity loss, which serve as powerful cautionary tales for those unfamiliar with these dynamics.

Workshops and community seminars can be organized to discuss the signs of cult involvement and the psychological tools used by these groups. Utilizing frameworks like the BITE Model—Behavior, Information, Thought, Emotion—can help participants understand how cults exert control over their members. Engaging discussions around these topics encourage critical thinking and equip attendees with skills to identify red flags such as authoritarian leadership or demands for absolute loyalty.

Moreover, leveraging digital platforms for educational outreach has become increasingly important in today's interconnected world. Social media campaigns can raise awareness about cult-related dangers while providing resources for those seeking help or information. Online forums can facilitate discussions among survivors and experts, creating a supportive environment where individuals feel safe to share their experiences and seek guidance.

In addition to formal education efforts, informal conversations within families and friend groups play a vital role in spreading awareness. Encouraging open dialogue about personal beliefs and values fosters an atmosphere where individuals feel comfortable discussing concerns related to potentially harmful groups.

Ultimately, educating others about the dangers associated with cults not only aids in individual protection but also contributes to building resilient communities capable of resisting manipulative influences. By prioritizing this education, we take significant steps toward safeguarding mental health and promoting critical thinking in our society.

12.2 Fostering Independence of Mind

Fostering independence of mind is a critical component in the prevention of cult involvement and other manipulative influences. This concept emphasizes the importance of nurturing critical thinking, self-awareness, and personal agency among individuals. By cultivating these traits, we empower people to make informed decisions and resist coercive tactics employed by high-control groups.

One effective approach to fostering independence is through education that encourages questioning and skepticism. Educational institutions can play a pivotal role by integrating curricula that promote analytical skills and ethical reasoning. For instance, courses in philosophy or debate can challenge students to explore diverse perspectives, thereby enhancing their ability to critically assess information rather than accepting it at face value.

Moreover, engaging in discussions about personal values and beliefs within families can significantly contribute to developing an independent mindset. Parents and guardians should create an environment where children feel safe expressing their thoughts and doubts. This open dialogue not only strengthens familial bonds but also equips young individuals with the confidence to voice their opinions against prevailing narratives they may encounter outside the home.

Community initiatives such as workshops focused on media literacy are also essential in this regard. In today's digital age, individuals are bombarded with information from various sources, making it crucial for them to discern credible content from misleading propaganda. Teaching skills like fact-checking and recognizing bias enables community members to navigate complex information landscapes effectively.

Additionally, promoting emotional intelligence plays a vital role in fostering independence of mind. Individuals who understand their emotions are better equipped to manage stressors that might lead them toward manipulative groups seeking vulnerable targets. Programs aimed at enhancing emotional resilience can help individuals develop coping strategies that reinforce their autonomy.

Ultimately, fostering independence of mind is about creating a culture that values critical thought over blind acceptance. By prioritizing education, open communication, media literacy, and emotional intelligence, we lay the groundwork for resilient individuals capable of resisting coercive influences while navigating life's complexities with confidence.

12.3 Promoting Skepticism Towards Manipulation

Promoting skepticism towards manipulation is essential in equipping individuals with the tools necessary to recognize and resist coercive influences. In a world increasingly characterized by misinformation and psychological manipulation, fostering a skeptical mindset can serve as a powerful defense against high-control groups and deceptive practices.

A critical aspect of promoting skepticism involves enhancing media literacy. As individuals navigate an information-rich environment, they must develop the ability to critically evaluate sources, discern biases, and identify manipulative tactics employed in various forms of communication. Educational programs that focus on analyzing news articles, advertisements, and social media content can empower individuals to question the motives behind the information presented to them.

Moreover, encouraging open dialogue about manipulation techniques can demystify these strategies and reduce their effectiveness. Workshops or community discussions that explore common psychological tactics—such as fear-mongering, emotional appeals, or social proof—can help participants recognize when they are being manipulated. By understanding these methods, individuals become more adept at questioning narratives that may seek to control their thoughts or behaviors.

Another vital component is fostering an environment where questioning is not only accepted but encouraged. Families and educational institutions should create spaces where curiosity thrives; this includes teaching children how to ask probing questions and think critically about authority figures or popular opinions. When young people learn that it is acceptable to challenge prevailing narratives respectfully, they are less likely to succumb to manipulative pressures later in life.

Additionally, promoting emotional intelligence plays a significant role in developing skepticism towards manipulation. Individuals who are attuned to their emotions can better recognize when they are being influenced by external pressures or emotional appeals. Programs aimed at enhancing self-awareness can help people understand their triggers and vulnerabilities, making them less susceptible to manipulative tactics.

Ultimately, promoting skepticism towards manipulation requires a multifaceted approach that combines education, open dialogue, and emotional awareness. By cultivating these skills within communities, we empower individuals not only to resist coercive influences but also to engage with the world around them thoughtfully and critically.

13 Resources for Further Reading

13.1 Support Networks for Survivors

Support networks play a crucial role in the recovery journey of individuals who have escaped cults. These networks provide not only emotional and psychological support but also practical resources that facilitate reintegration into society. Understanding the importance of these networks is essential for survivors as they navigate the complexities of healing from their experiences.

One significant aspect of support networks is the sense of community they foster among survivors. Many individuals exiting cults feel isolated and alienated due to their past experiences, which can lead to feelings of shame or confusion about their identity. Support groups, whether in-person or online, create safe spaces where survivors can share their stories without judgment. This shared understanding helps validate their experiences and fosters a sense of belonging that is often missing after leaving a cult.

Additionally, professional counseling services are integral to these support systems. Trained therapists who specialize in trauma and cult recovery can offer tailored strategies to help survivors process their experiences. Techniques such as cognitive-behavioral therapy (CBT) can assist individuals in reframing negative thought patterns instilled during their time in a cult, promoting healthier coping mechanisms moving forward.

- **Peer Support Groups:** These groups allow survivors to connect with others who have faced similar challenges, providing mutual encouragement and understanding.

- **Counseling Services:** Access to mental health professionals trained in trauma recovery is vital for addressing psychological scars left by cult involvement.

- **Educational Resources:** Workshops and seminars on critical thinking skills help empower survivors to rebuild their lives with confidence.

The role of advocacy organizations cannot be overlooked either; many provide resources specifically designed for former cult members. These organizations often offer hotlines, literature on recovery processes, and connections to legal assistance if needed. By leveraging these resources, survivors can reclaim agency over their lives while building resilience against potential future manipulative influences.

In conclusion, establishing robust support networks is essential for the healing journey of cult survivors. Through community connection, professional guidance, and access to educational resources, individuals can find pathways toward recovery that honor their unique experiences while fostering personal growth and empowerment.

13.2 Recommended Literature on Cults

The exploration of cults is a multifaceted subject that encompasses psychological, sociological, and historical perspectives. Understanding the dynamics of cults and their impact on individuals requires a comprehensive approach to literature that addresses these various dimensions. The recommended readings not only provide insights into the mechanisms of manipulation and control but also offer narratives of survival and recovery.

One seminal work in this field is "Cults in Our Midst" by Margaret Thaler Singer, which delves into the psychological tactics employed by cults to recruit and retain members. Singer's analysis is crucial for understanding how seemingly ordinary individuals can become ensnared in high-demand groups. Her emphasis on the importance of critical thinking skills serves as a foundation for those seeking to educate themselves about the signs of manipulative organizations.

Another important text is "Combatting Cult Mind Control" by Steven Hassan, a former member of the Moonies who has since dedicated his life to helping others escape similar situations. Hassan introduces his concept of the BITE model (Behavior, Information, Thought, and Emotional control), which provides a framework for analyzing how cults operate. His firsthand experiences lend authenticity to his insights, making this book both informative and relatable for readers.

"The Road to Freedom: Healing from Cult Abuse" by Dr. Janja Lalich offers an essential perspective on recovery from cult involvement. This book emphasizes not just understanding what happened within the cult but also outlines practical steps toward healing. Lalich's work highlights the importance of community support and professional guidance in reclaiming one's identity after leaving a controlling environment.

- **"Cults in Our Midst" by Margaret Thaler Singer:** A foundational text exploring psychological manipulation techniques used by cults.

- **"Combatting Cult Mind Control" by Steven Hassan:** Offers insights based on personal experience with a focus on recovery strategies.

- **"The Road to Freedom: Healing from Cult Abuse" by Dr. Janja Lalich:** Discusses pathways to healing post-cult involvement.

In addition to these key texts, numerous academic journals and articles provide ongoing research into cult dynamics and survivor experiences. Engaging with this literature equips readers with knowledge that fosters awareness and resilience against potential manipulative influences in society.

13.3 Glossary of Terms Related to the Topic

A comprehensive understanding of cults necessitates familiarity with specific terminology that encapsulates their dynamics, practices, and psychological impacts. This glossary serves as a foundational tool for readers seeking to navigate the complex landscape of cult studies, providing clarity on key concepts that are often encountered in literature and discussions surrounding this subject.

Cult: A group or movement exhibiting intense devotion to a leader or ideology, often characterized by manipulative practices and isolation from broader society. Cults typically employ high-pressure tactics to recruit and retain members.

High-demand group: A term used interchangeably with 'cult,' referring to organizations that impose strict behavioral controls on members, demanding total commitment and adherence to specific beliefs or practices.

Mind control: Techniques employed by cults to influence an individual's thoughts, emotions, and behaviors. This can include psychological manipulation strategies such as coercive persuasion, which aim to alter a person's worldview and sense of self.

BITE model: Developed by Steven Hassan, this framework categorizes the methods used by cults into four areas: Behavior control, Information control, Thought control, and Emotional control. Each component illustrates how cults maintain power over their members.

Cognitive dissonance: A psychological phenomenon where individuals experience discomfort due to conflicting beliefs or behaviors. In the context of cults, members may struggle with doubts about their involvement while simultaneously feeling compelled to conform.

Deprogramming: A process aimed at helping individuals exit a cult by challenging their indoctrinated beliefs and facilitating reintegration into mainstream society. This often involves therapeutic interventions designed to restore critical thinking skills.

Exit counseling: A supportive approach that assists former cult members in processing their experiences and rebuilding their lives outside the group. It emphasizes emotional healing and cognitive restructuring after leaving a high-demand environment.

This glossary not only aids in understanding the terminology associated with cult dynamics but also enhances awareness of the psychological mechanisms at play within these groups. By familiarizing oneself with these terms, readers can better engage with literature on the subject and recognize potential warning signs in various social contexts.

14 The Role of Family and Friends

14.1 Supporting Loved Ones Involved in a Cult

Supporting loved ones who are involved in a cult is a delicate and challenging endeavor that requires empathy, patience, and strategic communication. The emotional toll on family and friends can be significant, as they often feel helpless witnessing the changes in their loved ones. Understanding the psychological manipulation at play within cults is crucial for providing effective support.

One of the first steps in supporting someone involved in a cult is to educate oneself about the specific group and its practices. This knowledge allows family members to engage in informed conversations without appearing confrontational or dismissive. It's essential to approach discussions with an open mind, focusing on expressing concern rather than judgment. Phrasing questions thoughtfully can encourage dialogue; for instance, asking how they feel about certain teachings or practices can open pathways for reflection.

Establishing trust is vital when attempting to reconnect with someone entrenched in a cult environment. Regularly reaching out through phone calls, texts, or visits can help maintain a connection without overwhelming them. It's important to create a safe space where they feel comfortable sharing their experiences without fear of criticism or rejection. Listening actively and validating their feelings can foster this sense of safety.

Encouraging critical thinking is another key aspect of support. Gently prompting loved ones to question the beliefs and practices of the cult —without directly attacking those beliefs—can help them begin to see inconsistencies or manipulative tactics used by leaders. Providing alternative perspectives through books, articles, or documentaries about cult dynamics may also be beneficial.

In some cases, professional intervention may be necessary if the individual shows signs of severe psychological distress or if there are concerns for their safety. Engaging with mental health professionals who specialize in recovery from high-control groups can provide tailored strategies for both the individual and their support network.

Ultimately, patience is paramount; leaving a cult often involves complex emotional processes that take time. Family members should remain steadfastly supportive while respecting their loved one's autonomy throughout this journey toward recovery.

14.2 Communication Strategies for Concerned Individuals

Effective communication is essential when addressing the sensitive issue of a loved one involved in a cult. The strategies employed can significantly influence the outcome of these interactions, fostering understanding and potentially guiding the individual toward reconsidering their involvement. This section explores various communication techniques that can help concerned family members and friends navigate this challenging terrain.

One fundamental strategy is to adopt a non-confrontational approach. Instead of launching into accusations or expressing outright disapproval, individuals should focus on open-ended questions that encourage dialogue. For instance, asking "What do you find most fulfilling about your group?" allows the person to reflect on their experiences without feeling attacked. This method not only promotes conversation but also demonstrates genuine interest in their feelings and thoughts.

Active listening plays a crucial role in effective communication. By giving full attention to what the loved one is saying, concerned individuals can validate their emotions and experiences. Phrases like "I hear you" or "That sounds really important to you" can create an atmosphere of trust and safety, making it easier for the individual to share more openly about their beliefs and doubts.

Another vital aspect is sharing personal stories or experiences that relate to themes of manipulation or control without directly linking them to the cult experience. For example, discussing a time when one felt pressured by peers or society can subtly highlight similar dynamics present in cults, prompting reflection without direct confrontation.

Utilizing resources such as literature on cult dynamics can also be beneficial. Providing articles or books that discuss psychological manipulation in high-control groups may help individuals recognize patterns within their own situation. However, it's essential to introduce these materials gently—perhaps by suggesting they read something interesting rather than presenting them as evidence against the group.

Ultimately, patience remains key throughout this process. Change often takes time; therefore, maintaining consistent yet gentle communication reinforces support while respecting autonomy. By employing these strategies thoughtfully, concerned individuals can foster meaningful conversations that may lead their loved ones toward critical self-reflection and eventual liberation from harmful influences.

14.3 Building Trust with Those Affected

Building trust with individuals affected by cult involvement is a critical component in facilitating open dialogue and encouraging self-reflection. Trust serves as the foundation for any meaningful relationship, particularly when navigating the complexities of emotional and psychological manipulation that often characterize cult dynamics. Establishing this trust requires patience, empathy, and a strategic approach to communication.

One effective method for building trust is through consistent presence and availability. By being reliably present in the lives of those affected, family members and friends can demonstrate their commitment to supporting them without judgment. This consistent engagement fosters a sense of security, allowing individuals to feel safe enough to share their thoughts and feelings about their experiences within the group. For instance, regular check-ins or casual meet-ups can create opportunities for deeper conversations over time.

Another essential aspect is demonstrating understanding and compassion towards their situation. Acknowledging the emotional turmoil they may be experiencing can help bridge gaps in communication. Phrases like "I can't imagine how difficult this must be for you" validate their feelings while reinforcing that they are not alone in their struggles. This empathetic approach encourages individuals to lower their defenses, making them more receptive to discussions about their beliefs and experiences.

Moreover, sharing personal vulnerabilities can also enhance trust-building efforts. When concerned loved ones openly discuss their own challenges or past mistakes, it humanizes them and creates an environment where the affected individual feels less isolated in their struggles. This mutual sharing can lead to deeper connections that facilitate honest conversations about cult involvement.

Lastly, respecting autonomy is paramount in building trust. While it may be tempting to push for immediate change or intervention, recognizing an individual's right to make choices—even if those choices involve remaining within a cult—can foster respect and understanding. By prioritizing the individual's agency over coercive tactics, family members and friends can cultivate a trusting relationship that ultimately encourages self-exploration and critical thinking regarding their involvement.

15 Legal Perspectives on Cult Activity

15.1 Laws Surrounding Religious Freedom

The legal framework surrounding religious freedom is a cornerstone of democratic societies, ensuring that individuals can practice their beliefs without fear of persecution. This principle is particularly relevant when examining cults, as many operate under the guise of religious expression. Understanding these laws helps to delineate the fine line between legitimate religious practices and potentially harmful cult activities.

In many countries, constitutional protections for religious freedom are enshrined in law. For instance, the First Amendment of the United States Constitution guarantees citizens the right to freely exercise their religion while prohibiting Congress from establishing a religion. This dual protection creates a complex legal landscape where cults may exploit these freedoms to justify their actions, even when those actions may be harmful or coercive.

Internationally, various treaties and declarations also support religious freedom. The Universal Declaration of Human Rights asserts that everyone has the right to freedom of thought, conscience, and religion. However, interpretations of what constitutes acceptable religious practice can vary significantly across cultures and legal systems. This variance complicates efforts to regulate cults effectively without infringing on genuine expressions of faith.

Legal challenges often arise when cults engage in practices that conflict with public safety or individual rights. Courts have grappled with cases involving child custody disputes where one parent's involvement in a cult raises concerns about the welfare of children. Additionally, issues such as financial exploitation and psychological manipulation have led to calls for stricter regulations governing such groups.

Furthermore, anti-cult movements advocate for legislative measures aimed at protecting individuals from coercive persuasion techniques commonly employed by cults. These movements argue for clearer definitions within legal frameworks that distinguish between benign religious organizations and those that employ manipulative tactics detrimental to members' well-being.

Ultimately, navigating the intersection of religious freedom and cult activity requires careful consideration by lawmakers and society alike. Striking a balance between protecting individual rights and safeguarding against potential abuses remains an ongoing challenge in contemporary discourse surrounding faith-based organizations.

15.2 Legal Actions Against Abusive Practices

The legal landscape surrounding cults and their potentially abusive practices is complex and multifaceted. As societies become increasingly aware of the psychological, financial, and physical harm that can arise from cult activities, there has been a growing impetus for legal actions aimed at curbing these abuses. This section explores the various avenues through which individuals and communities can seek justice against harmful practices associated with cults.

One significant area of legal action involves civil lawsuits filed by former members or victims of cults. These lawsuits often allege fraud, emotional distress, or other forms of harm resulting from manipulative practices employed by cult leaders. For instance, in cases where individuals have been coerced into relinquishing their assets or subjected to psychological manipulation, courts may award damages to compensate for losses incurred. Such civil actions not only provide restitution to victims but also serve as a deterrent against future abuses by highlighting the consequences faced by exploitative organizations.

In addition to civil litigation, criminal charges can be pursued in instances where cult activities violate laws related to child welfare, human trafficking, or financial exploitation. Prosecutors may investigate allegations of abuse within cult settings—such as forced labor or sexual exploitation—and bring charges against perpetrators. High-profile cases have illustrated how law enforcement agencies can dismantle abusive networks operating under the guise of religious freedom while ensuring accountability for those who exploit vulnerable individuals.

Furthermore, advocacy groups play a crucial role in pushing for legislative reforms aimed at protecting individuals from coercive tactics commonly used by cults. These organizations often lobby for clearer definitions within existing laws that distinguish between legitimate religious practices and harmful behaviors masquerading as faith-based activities. By raising public awareness and influencing policy changes, these groups contribute significantly to creating a safer environment for potential victims.

Ultimately, the pursuit of legal actions against abusive practices within cults reflects society's commitment to safeguarding individual rights while navigating the delicate balance between religious freedom and protection from harm. As awareness grows regarding the dangers posed by certain groups operating under religious pretenses, it becomes imperative for lawmakers and advocates alike to continue refining legal frameworks that address these challenges effectively.

15.3 Advocacy for Victims' Rights

The advocacy for victims' rights in the context of cult activity is a critical aspect of addressing the harm inflicted by these organizations. As awareness grows regarding the psychological, emotional, and financial toll on individuals involved in cults, it becomes increasingly important to establish robust support systems that empower victims. This advocacy not only seeks justice for those affected but also aims to prevent future abuses through education and legislative reform.

One significant avenue for advocacy involves providing resources and support networks for former cult members. Organizations dedicated to this cause often offer counseling services, legal assistance, and community support groups that help individuals navigate their recovery journey. For instance, groups like the International Cultic Studies Association (ICSA) provide educational materials and connect survivors with mental health professionals who specialize in trauma related to cult experiences. Such initiatives are vital in helping victims reclaim their autonomy and rebuild their lives after leaving abusive environments.

Moreover, advocacy efforts extend into public policy realms where activists work tirelessly to influence legislation aimed at protecting potential victims from coercive practices. This includes lobbying for laws that enhance transparency within religious organizations and ensure accountability for harmful actions. By pushing for clearer definitions of what constitutes abusive behavior under the guise of religious freedom, advocates strive to create a legal framework that prioritizes individual rights while respecting genuine spiritual practices.

Additionally, raising public awareness about the tactics employed by cults is essential in preventing victimization. Educational campaigns can inform communities about warning signs associated with manipulative groups, thereby equipping individuals with knowledge that fosters resilience against coercive recruitment strategies. These efforts can be particularly impactful when integrated into school curricula or community workshops, ensuring that people are better prepared to recognize and resist such influences.

In conclusion, advocacy for victims' rights plays a pivotal role in addressing the complex challenges posed by cult activities. By fostering supportive environments, influencing policy changes, and promoting public education on these issues, advocates contribute significantly to safeguarding individual freedoms while holding exploitative organizations accountable.

16 Cultural Representations of Cults

16.1 Media Portrayals and Their Impact

The portrayal of cults in media plays a significant role in shaping public perception and understanding of these often-misunderstood groups. From sensationalized documentaries to fictional narratives, the representation of cults can influence societal attitudes, instill fear, or even foster curiosity about their inner workings. This section explores how various forms of media contribute to the cultural narrative surrounding cults and the implications of these portrayals on individuals and communities.

Media representations frequently emphasize extreme behaviors and tragic outcomes associated with cults, such as mass suicides or violent confrontations. These depictions can lead to a skewed understanding that all cults are dangerous, overshadowing the more nuanced realities of many groups that may not engage in harmful practices. For instance, films like "The Master" or series such as "Wild Wild Country" dramatize real events but often prioritize entertainment over accuracy, potentially perpetuating stereotypes that stigmatize those involved in alternative spiritual movements.

Moreover, news coverage tends to focus on high-profile cases like Jonestown or Waco, which can create a sense of urgency around the need for intervention against perceived threats posed by cults. This framing can result in increased scrutiny and suspicion towards unconventional religious practices or communal living arrangements that do not conform to mainstream norms. As a consequence, individuals who might benefit from exploring alternative belief systems may feel deterred due to fear of being labeled as part of a 'cult.'

On social media platforms, discussions about cults often take on viral characteristics where misinformation can spread rapidly. Memes and short videos may trivialize serious issues related to manipulation and psychological control within these groups. Such content risks desensitizing audiences to the genuine struggles faced by former members while simultaneously glamorizing the allure of belonging to an exclusive community.

In conclusion, while media portrayals serve as a lens through which society views cults, they also carry significant responsibility for fostering informed dialogue versus sensationalism. Understanding this impact is crucial for developing critical thinking skills regarding how we interpret stories about cults—both in fiction and reality—and recognizing the potential consequences these narratives have on individuals seeking connection outside conventional frameworks.

16.2 Literature Depicting Cult Experiences

The exploration of cult experiences in literature serves as a powerful medium for understanding the complexities and nuances surrounding these often-misunderstood groups. Through fictional narratives, autobiographies, and critical essays, authors provide insights into the psychological, social, and emotional dimensions of life within cults. This literary representation not only reflects individual experiences but also contributes to broader societal discussions about belief systems, manipulation, and the quest for belonging.

One significant aspect of literature depicting cult experiences is its ability to humanize individuals who may otherwise be viewed through a lens of stigma or fear. Works such as "Educated" by Tara Westover offer poignant accounts of growing up in a strict ideological environment that can be likened to a cult. Westover's narrative illustrates the struggle between familial loyalty and personal autonomy, shedding light on the internal conflicts faced by those raised in such settings. Similarly, "The Girls" by Emma Cline presents a fictionalized account inspired by the Manson Family, exploring themes of vulnerability and seduction within cult dynamics.

Moreover, literature often delves into the psychological mechanisms at play within cults—such as coercive persuasion and identity transformation. In "The Road to Jonestown," author Jeff Guinn provides an investigative perspective on Jim Jones and his followers while examining how charismatic leadership can manipulate collective beliefs. This type of analysis encourages readers to reflect critically on their own belief systems and the factors that influence them.

Additionally, literary portrayals frequently highlight the aftermath of leaving a cult—an experience fraught with challenges such as reintegration into society and grappling with lost relationships. Novels like "The Sound of Things Falling" by Juan Gabriel Vásquez illustrate how past affiliations can haunt individuals long after they have distanced themselves from harmful ideologies. These narratives foster empathy towards former members while emphasizing the importance of support systems during recovery.

In conclusion, literature depicting cult experiences plays a crucial role in shaping public perception by offering diverse perspectives that challenge stereotypes associated with these groups. By engaging with these texts, readers gain deeper insights into the complexities of human behavior related to faith, community, and personal freedom.

16.3 Film and Television Representations

The portrayal of cults in film and television serves as a significant cultural lens through which audiences can explore the complexities of belief systems, manipulation, and the human psyche. These visual mediums often dramatize real-life events or fictional narratives that resonate with societal fears and fascinations surrounding cults. By examining these representations, we gain insights into how media shapes public perception and understanding of such groups.

One notable aspect of film and television representations is their ability to evoke emotional responses from viewers. Films like "Midsommar" delve into the psychological horror associated with cult dynamics, showcasing how individuals can be seduced by seemingly idyllic communities that harbor dark secrets. The cinematography and narrative structure create an immersive experience that reflects the allure and danger of cult life, prompting viewers to question their own beliefs about community and belonging.

Television series such as "The Path" provide a more nuanced exploration of cult experiences by focusing on character development and moral dilemmas faced by members. This series illustrates the internal conflicts between loyalty to a group and personal autonomy, allowing audiences to empathize with characters who grapple with their identities within a controlling environment. Such portrayals challenge stereotypes by presenting multifaceted individuals rather than one-dimensional caricatures.

Moreover, documentaries like "Wild Wild Country" offer real-life accounts of controversial figures like Bhagwan Shree Rajneesh, highlighting the complexities involved in cult leadership and follower dynamics. These documentaries not only inform but also provoke critical discussions about power, charisma, and the impact of charismatic leaders on vulnerable individuals seeking purpose or community.

In conclusion, film and television representations of cults play a crucial role in shaping societal narratives around these groups. By engaging with diverse portrayals—from horror films to character-driven dramas—viewers are encouraged to reflect on broader themes such as manipulation, identity crisis, and the quest for belonging. Ultimately, these visual stories contribute significantly to our understanding of human behavior in relation to faith-based communities.

17 Future Trends in Understanding Cults

17.1 Evolving Definitions in Society

The understanding of cults has undergone significant transformation over the years, reflecting broader societal changes and evolving psychological insights. As our cultural landscape shifts, so too does the language we use to describe groups that exhibit cult-like characteristics. This evolution is crucial for recognizing the nuances between harmful organizations and benign communities, which can often be misclassified.

Historically, the term "cult" was predominantly associated with fringe religious movements that deviated from mainstream beliefs. However, contemporary definitions have expanded to encompass a variety of groups, including political factions and self-help organizations that employ manipulative tactics. This shift highlights the need for a more inclusive framework that considers not only religious but also ideological and psychological dimensions of influence.

One significant factor contributing to this evolving definition is the increasing awareness of psychological manipulation techniques used by these groups. The BITE Model—Behavior, Information, Thought, Emotion—serves as a critical tool in identifying how cults exert control over their members. By understanding these mechanisms, society can better differentiate between healthy group dynamics and those that are exploitative or coercive.

Moreover, real-life stories of individuals who have escaped such environments underscore the importance of recognizing subtle signs of cultic behavior beyond traditional definitions. For instance, many modern-day cults utilize digital platforms for recruitment and community building, complicating our understanding further. The rise of social media has created echo chambers where misinformation thrives and individuals become increasingly isolated from dissenting viewpoints.

This evolving perspective on what constitutes a cult emphasizes the necessity for ongoing education about these dynamics within society. As definitions continue to adapt to new contexts—such as online interactions—the importance of critical thinking skills becomes paramount in safeguarding against potential manipulation. By fostering an environment where questioning authority is encouraged and diverse perspectives are valued, society can mitigate the risks associated with cult-like influences.

17.2 Potential New Forms of Manipulative Groups

The emergence of new forms of manipulative groups is a pressing concern in our rapidly evolving social landscape. As technology advances and societal norms shift, these groups adapt their strategies to exploit vulnerabilities in individuals and communities. Understanding these potential new forms is crucial for developing effective countermeasures against manipulation.

One significant trend is the rise of online cults, which leverage digital platforms to recruit and maintain followers. These groups often utilize social media algorithms that create echo chambers, reinforcing members' beliefs while isolating them from dissenting opinions. For instance, some wellness communities may promote extreme health regimens or pseudoscientific practices under the guise of holistic living, leading individuals to abandon conventional medical advice in favor of unverified treatments.

Another emerging form involves political extremism, where groups employ manipulative tactics to radicalize individuals. These organizations often use fear-based messaging and misinformation campaigns to create a sense of urgency around perceived threats. By fostering an "us versus them" mentality, they can effectively mobilize followers towards extremist actions or ideologies. The recent surge in conspiracy theory movements exemplifies this phenomenon, as they attract individuals seeking belonging and purpose amidst societal uncertainty.

Additionally, self-help movements have evolved into potentially manipulative entities that exploit personal vulnerabilities for profit. Some programs promise transformative experiences but may employ high-pressure sales tactics or emotional manipulation to retain participants and maximize revenue. This commodification of personal growth can lead individuals down a path where financial investment becomes synonymous with self-worth, creating dependency on the group for validation.

As we navigate these complexities, it becomes increasingly important to foster critical thinking skills within society. Education systems should emphasize media literacy and psychological resilience to equip individuals with the tools necessary to recognize manipulative behaviors across various contexts—be it online forums or local community gatherings. By promoting awareness and encouraging open dialogue about these issues, we can better protect ourselves from the insidious nature of modern manipulative groups.

17.3 The Importance of Ongoing Research

Ongoing research into cults and manipulative groups is essential for several reasons, particularly as these entities evolve in response to societal changes and technological advancements. Understanding the dynamics of these groups not only aids in identifying their tactics but also equips individuals and communities with the knowledge necessary to resist manipulation.

One critical aspect of ongoing research is its role in uncovering new methodologies employed by cults. As highlighted previously, the rise of online platforms has transformed traditional recruitment strategies. Researchers must continuously analyze how social media algorithms can create echo chambers that reinforce harmful ideologies. By studying these patterns, scholars can develop effective counter-narratives that promote critical thinking and resilience among potential targets.

Moreover, ongoing research contributes to a deeper understanding of the psychological mechanisms at play within cults. Investigating how emotional manipulation, fear tactics, and groupthink operate allows for the development of educational programs aimed at enhancing individual awareness. For instance, workshops focused on recognizing coercive persuasion techniques can empower individuals to make informed decisions about their affiliations and beliefs.

The importance of interdisciplinary collaboration cannot be overstated in this context. Psychologists, sociologists, technologists, and educators must work together to create comprehensive frameworks that address the multifaceted nature of modern cults. This collaborative approach can lead to innovative solutions tailored to specific demographics or community needs, ensuring that interventions are both relevant and effective.

Additionally, ongoing research fosters public discourse around the implications of manipulative groups on society as a whole. By disseminating findings through various media channels—academic publications, documentaries, or community seminars—researchers can raise awareness about the dangers posed by these organizations. This heightened awareness encourages proactive measures from policymakers and community leaders aimed at safeguarding vulnerable populations.

In conclusion, continuous investigation into cult dynamics is vital for developing robust defenses against manipulation in an increasingly complex world. By prioritizing this area of study, we not only protect individuals but also contribute to a more informed society capable of resisting coercive influences.

18 Final Thoughts on Vigilance

18.1 Staying Alert to Manipulative Practices

In an era where information is abundant yet often misleading, staying alert to manipulative practices is crucial for personal autonomy and mental well-being. Cults and similar organizations thrive on the vulnerabilities of individuals, employing sophisticated psychological tactics that can ensnare even the most discerning minds. Understanding these manipulative practices not only aids in recognizing potential threats but also empowers individuals to maintain their critical thinking skills.

One of the primary techniques used by cults is emotional manipulation, which can manifest through various strategies such as love bombing—where new recruits are showered with affection and attention to create a sense of belonging. This initial warmth can obscure the underlying control mechanisms that will later be employed. As members become more entrenched, they may experience isolation from outside influences, further solidifying their dependency on the group.

Another significant aspect of manipulation involves controlling information. Cults often restrict access to external viewpoints, creating echo chambers that reinforce their doctrines while discrediting dissenting opinions. This tactic not only limits critical engagement but also fosters an environment where questioning becomes synonymous with betrayal. Recognizing this pattern is essential; individuals must actively seek diverse perspectives to counteract this form of control.

The use of guilt and fear as tools for compliance cannot be overlooked either. Members may be made to feel responsible for the group's success or failure, leading them to suppress doubts or concerns about their involvement. This psychological burden can result in profound internal conflict and distress, making it imperative for individuals to identify these feelings early on.

Ultimately, vigilance against manipulative practices requires ongoing self-reflection and a commitment to maintaining one's independence of thought. By cultivating awareness and resilience against these tactics, individuals can protect themselves from becoming unwitting participants in harmful systems.

To combat these manipulative practices effectively, fostering a culture of open dialogue and skepticism is vital. Encouraging discussions about personal experiences and beliefs can help illuminate potential red flags associated with coercive groups. Additionally, educating oneself about common manipulation tactics equips individuals with the knowledge necessary to recognize when they or someone they care about might be falling prey to such influences.

18.2 Encouraging Open Dialogue About Beliefs

Encouraging open dialogue about beliefs is essential in fostering a culture of critical thinking and resilience against manipulative practices. In an age where misinformation can spread rapidly, creating safe spaces for discussion allows individuals to explore their thoughts and feelings without fear of judgment or reprisal. This openness not only promotes personal growth but also strengthens community bonds by encouraging diverse perspectives.

One effective approach to facilitating these conversations is through structured forums or discussion groups that focus on various belief systems, including religious, political, and philosophical ideologies. These gatherings can serve as platforms for individuals to share their experiences and challenge each other's viewpoints respectfully. By engaging in such dialogues, participants learn to articulate their beliefs clearly while also developing the ability to listen actively and empathize with differing opinions.

Moreover, educational institutions play a pivotal role in promoting open dialogue about beliefs. Incorporating curricula that emphasize critical thinking skills and the examination of multiple viewpoints prepares students to navigate complex social landscapes. Workshops that teach conflict resolution and communication strategies can further equip individuals with the tools necessary for constructive discussions, enabling them to address disagreements without resorting to hostility.

In addition to formal settings, informal conversations among friends and family are equally important. Encouraging loved ones to express their beliefs openly fosters an environment where questioning becomes a natural part of discourse rather than a taboo subject. This familial support system can be crucial when individuals encounter manipulative groups; having trusted allies who understand their values can provide a buffer against coercive influences.

Ultimately, promoting open dialogue about beliefs cultivates an atmosphere of trust and understanding within communities. It empowers individuals to critically assess their convictions while remaining vigilant against manipulation. By embracing this practice, society can build resilience against harmful ideologies and encourage a more informed citizenry capable of navigating the complexities of modern life.

18.3 Commitment to Education and Awareness

The commitment to education and awareness is a cornerstone in the fight against manipulation and misinformation. In an era where information is abundant yet often misleading, fostering a culture of informed citizens becomes imperative. This commitment not only empowers individuals but also fortifies communities against harmful ideologies that thrive on ignorance.

Education serves as the primary tool for equipping individuals with critical thinking skills necessary for discerning fact from fiction. By integrating media literacy into educational curricula, students learn to analyze sources critically, question narratives, and recognize biases in information dissemination. For instance, programs that teach students how to evaluate news articles or social media posts can significantly reduce susceptibility to misinformation. Such initiatives encourage a proactive approach to consuming information rather than passive acceptance.

Moreover, awareness campaigns play a vital role in reaching broader audiences beyond traditional educational settings. Community workshops, public seminars, and online webinars can effectively disseminate knowledge about common manipulative tactics used by various groups. These platforms provide opportunities for individuals to engage with experts who can share insights on recognizing red flags associated with coercive practices. For example, discussions around psychological manipulation techniques can empower attendees to identify when they or their loved ones may be targeted.

In addition to formal education and community outreach, fostering a culture of lifelong learning is essential. Encouraging curiosity and open-mindedness allows individuals to continuously seek knowledge throughout their lives. Libraries, online courses, and discussion forums serve as valuable resources for ongoing education. When people commit themselves to learning about diverse perspectives—be it through literature, documentaries, or podcasts—they become more resilient against dogmatic beliefs that may lead them astray.

Ultimately, the commitment to education and awareness cultivates an informed citizenry capable of navigating complex societal issues with discernment and empathy. By prioritizing these values within communities and institutions alike, society can build a robust defense against manipulation while promoting understanding across differing viewpoints.

References:

• Langone, M. D. (1993). *Recovery from Cults: Help for Victims of Psychological and Spiritual Abuse*. W.W. Norton & Company.

• Bromley, D. G. (2007). *The Psychology of Religious Cults*. In The Cambridge Handbook of Sociology.

• Stark, R., & Bainbridge, W. S. (1985). *The Future of Religion: Secularization, Revival and Cult Formation*. University of California Press.

• Hassan, S. (2000). *Releasing the Bonds: Empowering People to Think for Themselves*. Freedom of Mind Press.

• Lalich, J. (2004). *Take Back Your Life: Recovering from Cults and Abusive Relationships*. New Page Books.

• West, D. (2015). The Cult Recovery Handbook: A Guide to Healing from Psychological Manipulation.

• Pennycook, G., & Rand, D. G. (2018). Fighting misinformation on social media using crowdsourced judgments of news source quality. Proceedings of the National Academy of Sciences.

• Wineburg, S., & McGrew, S. (2019). Lateral Reading and the Nature of Expertise: How Trustworthy is the Internet?

• Bromley, D. G., & Melton, J. G. (2002). *Cult Awareness and Education: A Guide for Parents and Educators*. The American Psychological Association.

• Hobbs, R. (2010). Digital and Media Literacy: A Plan of Action. Aspen Institute.

• Lofland, J., & Stark, R. (1965). Becoming a World-Saver: A Theory of Conversion to a Deviant Perspective.

• Janis, I.L. (1972). Victims of Groupthink: A Psychological Study of Foreign-Policy Decisions and Fiascoes.

• Del Vicario, M., et al. (2016). "Echo Chambers in Social Media: A Case Study of the Italian Political Debate." Proceedings of the National Academy of Sciences.

• Tufekci, Z. (2017). "Twitter and Tear Gas: The Power and Fragility of Networked Protest." Yale University Press.

• Cialdini, R.B.(2006) *.Influence: The Psychology of Persuasion.* Harper Business.

BOOKS BY THIS AUTHOR

Gemeinsam den Weg gehen: Empathie im Umgang mit psychischen Erkrankungen für Angehörige und Patienten (Psychotherapie: Mittel und Methoden)

Psychische Erkrankungen sind komplex und vielschichtig. Sie können das Leben der Betroffenen und ihrer Angehörigen stark beeinflussen. In diesem Buch wird auf die Bedeutung von Empathie im Umgang mit psychischen Erkrankungen aufmerksam gemacht und gezeigt, wie Angehörige und Patienten gemeinsam zu einem guten Umgang finden können.

The Battle Within: A Guide to Overcoming Inner Struggles

"The Battle Within: A Guide to Overcoming Inner Struggles" is a profound and insightful guide designed to help readers navigate the complex landscape of inner struggles. This eBook delves into the psychological aspects of personal conflicts, offering readers a deep understanding of the forces shaping their internal experiences.

In this transformative journey, readers will discover the crucial role of childhood experiences, societal influences, and personal beliefs in forming their current challenges.

The book emphasizes the importance of communication and boundary-setting as tools for managing these struggles, providing practical advice and strategies to apply in everyday life.

Each chapter is a step towards self-discovery and healing, addressing common emotional battles such as anxiety and depression, and guiding readers towards fostering healthier relationships. This guide is not just about overcoming difficulties; it's about empowering individuals to make significant, positive changes in their lives.

Whether you're seeking to understand the roots of your inner conflicts or looking for ways to foster your personal growth, "The Battle Within" offers a compassionate, insightful, and practical approach to achieving emotional well-being and self-empowerment.

Dankbarkeit im Alltag: Ein interaktives Tagebuch für mehr Zufriedenheit und Lebensfreude

Tauchen Sie ein in die Welt der Dankbarkeit und erleben Sie, wie sie Ihr Leben positiv verändern kann. "Dankbarkeit im Alltag: Ein interaktives Tagebuch für mehr Zufriedenheit und Lebensfreude" ist Ihr interaktiver Begleiter auf einer inspirierenden Reise der Selbstreflexion und des Wohlbefindens.

In diesem einfühlsamen eBook lädt Sie der Diplom-Psychologe und Psychologische Psychotherapeut Dirk Werner ein, die transformative Kraft der Dankbarkeit zu entdecken. Beginnen Sie eine Reise der Selbstentdeckung, während Sie lernen, die kleinen Freuden des Lebens zu schätzen und Ihre Perspektive auf das Positive zu lenken.

Was Sie erwartet:

• Verständnis der Bedeutung von Dankbarkeit und wie sie Ihr Leben bereichern kann.

• Wissenschaftliche Einblicke und Studien, die die Vorteile der Dankbarkeit auf psychisches und physisches Wohlbefinden untermauern.

• Praktische Übungen und Inspirationen, um Dankbarkeit in Ihren Alltag zu integrieren.

• Persönliche Erfolgsgeschichten und Fallstudien, die zeigen, wie Dankbarkeit Leben verändert hat.

• Reflexionsfragen und Raum für Ihre eigenen Gedanken und Ziele.

• Empfehlungen für weiterführende Literatur und die Möglichkeit, sich mit einer Dankbarkeits-Community zu verbinden.

• Inspirierende Zitate und Geschichten, die Ihr Herz erwärmen werden.

"Dankbarkeit im Alltag" ist mehr als nur ein Buch; es ist Ihr interaktives Tagebuch, um ein erfülltes und dankbares Leben zu führen. Es ermutigt Sie, sich täglich auf das Gute zu konzentrieren und eine tiefe Dankbarkeit für das zu entwickeln, was Sie haben.

Entdecken Sie die Magie der Dankbarkeit und starten Sie Ihre Reise zu mehr Zufriedenheit und Lebensfreude im Alltag noch heute!

Suizidprävention - Basics

Suizid ist eine globale Tragödie, von der jährlich Hunderttausende Menschen betroffen sind. Doch es gibt Hoffnung! Dieses Dokument beleuchtet, welche Faktoren die Suizidgefahr erhöhen und was wir dagegen tun können.

Erfahren Sie, warum psychische Erkrankungen, Suchtprobleme und frühere Versuche das Risiko drastisch steigern. Entdecken Sie, wie der Zugang zu Therapie und Unterstützungsnetzwerken Menschen vor dem Schlimmsten bewahren kann.

Eine Vielzahl praktischer Präventionsstrategien wird vorgestellt - von gezielten Interventionen für Hochrisiko-Gruppen bis hin zu großangelegten Aufklärungskampagnen. Verschaffen Sie sich einen Überblick über dringend benötigte Lösungsansätze.

Es ist an der Zeit zu handeln und Menschenleben zu retten. Lassen Sie sich von dieser fundierten Zusammenfassung über Suizidprävention inspirieren und motivieren. Gemeinsam können wir Suizid entgegenwirken!

Leben retten durch Wissen und Handeln: Erfahren Sie, welche Faktoren das Risiko für Suizidversuche erhöhen und was effektiv dagegen unternommen werden kann. Dieses fundierte Dokument beleuchtet Präventionsansätze, die Leben retten können. Lassen Sie sich inspirieren! Gemeinsam können wir Suizid entgegenwirken und Menschen vor dieser tödlichen Tragödie bewahren. Entdecken Sie Lösungsansätze für ein sensibles, aber hochaktuelles Thema.

101 goldene Regeln für eine harmonische Paar-Beziehung

Liebe auf Dauer ist eine tägliche Entscheidung und Übung. Doch wie schafft man es, dass die Zweisamkeit nicht im Alltag untergeht? Wie hält man die Flamme der Leidenschaft am Brennen und überwindet selbst schwierige Phasen?

In "101 goldene Regeln für eine harmonische Paar-Beziehung" gibt Ihnen der erfahrene Paartherapeut Dirk Werner wertvolle Impulse an die Hand. Ob romantische Gesten, erneuerte Traditionen oder wichtige Verhaltensweisen - hier finden Sie unzählige erprobte Möglichkeiten, um Ihrer Partnerschaft neuen Schwung zu verleihen.

Lernen Sie mit einfachen, aber wirkungsvollen Schritten und Ritualen die pure Magie des Verliebtseins wiederaufblühen zu lassen. Holen Sie sich Inspiration für unvergessliche Zweisamkeit, erotische Abenteuer und tiefes Vertrauen. Erfahren Sie, wie eine offene und wertschätzende Kommunikation gelingt und warum gemeinsam verbrachte Zeit so wichtig ist.

Dieses Buch ist ein wertvoller Begleiter für Paare, die ihre Liebe auffrischen und ihre Verbindung auf eine neue Ebene heben möchten. Machen Sie sich auf den Weg zu einer leidenschaftlichen und stets blühenden Beziehung!

Holen Sie sich jetzt die idealen Rezepte für dauerhafte Zweisamkeit und tiefe Verbundenheit!

Malen gegen den Schmerz" der Schlüssel zu deiner inneren Heilung

Finde inneren Frieden durch die Kraft der Kreativität

Fühlst du dich von Schmerzen, Ängsten oder traumatischen Erlebnissen belastet? Suchst du nach einem Weg, um diese Gefühle auf heilsame Weise zu verarbeiten? Dann ist "Malen gegen den Schmerz" der Schlüssel zu deiner inneren Heilung.

In diesem einzigartigen Buch entdeckst du, wie du die transformative Kraft des kreativen Malens nutzen kannst, um deine Emotionen auszudrücken und Traumata zu bewältigen. Durch praxisnahe Übungen, berührende Beschreibungen und über 50 sorgfältig gestaltete Malvorlagen lernst du Schritt für Schritt, wie du den Malprozess als Weg der Selbstreflexion nutzen kannst.

Psychotherapeut und Autor Dirk Werner führt dich behutsam durch die Welt der Farben, Formen und künstlerischen Ausdrucksmöglichkeiten. Du erfährst, wie du achtsam mit deinen Gefühlen in Kontakt trittst und sie dann auf die Leinwand bringst. Jeder Pinselstrich wird zu einer Botschaft deiner Seele, einer Einladung zur Heilung.

Entdecke die therapeutische Wirkung des Malens als kraftvolles Instrument zur Traumabewältigung. Sei mutig und lasse die Kreativität in dir erwachen! Erschaffe Kunstwerke, die den Ausdruck deines wahren Selbst spiegeln und dich auf eine transformative Reise zu neuem Selbstvertrauen und Lebensmut führen.

Ob du ganz am Anfang deines Heilungsweges stehst oder einfach neue Inspirationen für deine künstlerische Praxis suchst - "Malen gegen den Schmerz" ist dein Begleiter zu mehr Ausgeglichenheit, Resilienz und innerer Stärke.

Kosmische Matrix: Heilige Geometrie zum Ausmalen 70+ inspirierende Motive

'Kosmische Matrix' eröffnet Ihnen die faszinierende Welt der heiligen Geometrie. Dieses einzigartige Ausmalbuch ist ein Portal zu den grundlegenden Mustern des Universums. Auf jeder Seite erwarten Sie sorgfältig gestaltete geometrische Formen, die uralte Prinzipien mit modernen kosmologischen Konzepten verbinden.

Von der Blume des Lebens und dem Goldenen Schnitt über Tiere, Gesichter, Natur- und Fantasielandschaften bis zu komplexen Fraktalen - Ihre Kreativität kennt keine Grenzen, wenn Sie diese zeitlosen Designs mit Farbe zum Leben erwecken. 'Kosmische Matrix' geht über ein gewöhnliches Ausmalbuch hinaus; es ist eine meditative Reise durch die Strukturen unserer Realität und darüber hinaus.

Entdecken Sie die Harmonie zwischen Mikrokosmos und Makrokosmos, während Sie Ihre eigene farbenfrohe Interpretation der kosmischen Ordnung erschaffen. Perfekt für Liebhaber der Heiligen Geometrie, Kunstenthusiasten und alle, die nach einer entspannenden, doch tiefsinnigen kreativen Auszeit suchen.

Selbstsabotage überwinden: Entfessle dein wahres Potenzial

Fühlst du dich manchmal, als wärst du dein eigener schlimmster Feind? Stehst du dir selbst im Weg, wenn es darum geht, deine Ziele zu erreichen? Du bist nicht allein.

In diesem bahnbrechenden eBook enthüllt der Psychologische Psychotherapeut und Autor Dirk Werner die verborgenen Mechanismen der Selbstsabotage und bietet praxiserprobte Strategien, um sie ein für alle Mal zu überwinden. Basierend auf jahrzehntelanger psychologischer Forschung und persönlicher professioneller Erfahrung zeigt dieses Buch dir, wie du:

- Die Wurzeln deiner Selbstsabotage erkennst und verstehst
- Effektive Techniken zur Zielsetzung und -erreichung meisterst
- Innere Konflikte auflöst und deine Motivation steuerst
- Dein Selbstvertrauen stärkst und negative Glaubenssätze überwindest
- Dauerhafte Veränderungen in deinem Leben herbeiführst

Dieses eBook ist mehr als nur ein Ratgeber – es ist dein persönlicher Wegweiser zur Selbstentdeckung und zum Erfolg. Mit einer Mischung aus wissenschaftlichen Erkenntnissen, praktischen Übungen und inspirierenden Geschichten wirst du lernen, wie du deinen inneren "Zieljäger" erweckst und dein volles Potenzial entfaltest.

Egal ob du deine Karriere vorantreiben, deine Beziehungen verbessern oder einfach ein erfüllteres Leben führen möchtest – "Selbstsabotage überwinden" gibt dir die Werkzeuge an die Hand, die du brauchst, um deine Träume Wirklichkeit werden zu lassen.

Bist du bereit, die Fesseln der Selbstsabotage zu sprengen und dein bestes Selbst zu werden? Dann ist dieses eBook genau das Richtige für dich. Lade es jetzt herunter und beginne deine Reise zur Selbstverwirklichung!

Perfekt für:

- Berufstätige, die ihre Karriere auf die nächste Stufe heben wollen
- Studierende, die ihre akademische Leistung verbessern möchten
- Unternehmer, die ihre Geschäfte ausbauen wollen
- Jeden, der persönliches Wachstum und Erfolg anstrebt

Entfessle dein wahres Potenzial – heute!

Self-Love Over Perfection: A Guide to Overcoming Female Narcissism

Are you exhausted by the relentless chase for perfection and the constant need for validation? Self-Love Over Perfection is your compassionate companion on the journey to self-acceptance and emotional freedom. Dive deep into the unique traits of female narcissism, uncover the societal and psychological roots, and discover transformative strategies to build genuine self-esteem and authentic relationships. ◈◈

What You'll Find Inside:

Understanding Female Narcissism: Gain profound insights into the specific characteristics of female narcissism and how it differs from male narcissism. Learn how societal pressures, cultural expectations, and psychological factors contribute to these behaviors.

Real-Life Stories and Case Studies: Read inspiring stories of women who have faced and overcome their narcissistic tendencies. Their journeys offer hope, motivation, and practical lessons.

Practical Exercises and Tools: Access a wealth of practical exercises, self-reflection prompts, and actionable steps designed to help you cultivate self-love, resilience, and a healthier self-esteem.

Therapeutic Insights: Discover evidence-based therapeutic approaches and techniques that can guide you through your healing process. Learn when and how to seek professional help, and explore the benefits of support groups and online communities.

Building Authentic Relationships: Develop skills to foster genuine connections with others. Learn the importance of empathy, vulnerability, and setting healthy boundaries in your relationships.

Why This Book Is For You:

Whether you identify with narcissistic traits, are a therapist seeking to better support your clients, or simply want to help a loved one, Self-Love Over Perfection provides the guidance and support you need. This book is a beacon of hope and a source of strength, offering a clear path towards emotional healing and self-empowerment.

Join the Journey:

Embark on a transformative journey of self-discovery and growth. Embrace your true self, let go of the need for perfection, and cultivate a healthier self-esteem. Remember, you are enough just as you are. ◈

Nanogenesis: The Rise of Superhumans

In the gripping science fiction thriller "Nanogenesis: The Rise of Superhumans", humanity stands on the brink of a revolutionary breakthrough in nanotechnology. Set in a near-future world where technology seamlessly integrates with human biology, this novel explores the ethical, societal, and existential dilemmas that arise from such advancements.

The story unfolds in Neo-Tokyo, a city rebuilt with advanced bio-nano architecture, creating an environment where technology is indistinguishable from nature. Here, skyscrapers mimic photosynthesis, and streets self-repair through nano-assemblers. However, beneath this utopian veneer lies a brewing conflict between those who embrace these enhancements and those who view them as an abomination to human identity.

At the heart of the narrative is Dr. Eliana Moraes, a brilliant nanotechnologist driven by her quest to eradicate diseases using her groundbreaking nano-augmentations. Her creation promises superhuman abilities and immortality but also poses significant risks which she struggles to contain. Accompanying Eliana is her former mentor turned antagonist, Dr. Felix Brehm, whose vision for humanity's future clashes violently with hers. He believes in using nanotechnology for augmenting humans into superior beings, leading to a dangerous ideological war. As Eliana races against time to prevent misuse of her technology that could lead to an elite class of superhumans dominating the ordinary, she faces internal conflicts about her role in potentially altering the course of evolution. The tension escalates when a radical group seeks to steal her research to create an unstoppable army.

"Nanogenesis: The Rise of Superhumans" delves deep into themes of power, control versus freedom, and the moral implications of playing god. Through its complex characters and intricate plot twists—such as unexpected alliances and betrayals—the book keeps readers on edge while prompting them to ponder profound questions about progress and identity.

Targeted towards fans of speculative fiction who relish cerebral narratives intertwined with action-packed sequences, this novel combines scientific plausibility with rich storytelling to craft a world both visionary and eerily familiar.

Der Herzschmerz-Ratgeber: Eine Schritt-für-Schritt-Anleitung zur Heilung und zum Neuanfang

Herzschmerz - ein Gefühl, das viele von uns kennen. Es ist ein Zustand, der durch eine Trennung, einen Verlust oder eine Enttäuschung ausgelöst wird und uns oft hilflos und allein zurücklässt. Doch es gibt Hoffnung! Dieses Buch bietet eine praktische und einfühlsame Anleitung, um Ihren Herzschmerz zu überwinden und einen Neuanfang zu wagen.

In diesem Buch werden Sie lernen, wie Sie Ihre Gefühle akzeptieren und verarbeiten können, wie Sie loslassen und sich auf ein neues Leben konzentrieren können. Sie werden entdecken, wie Sie Ihre körperliche und geistige Gesundheit verbessern können, wie Sie Unterstützung finden und wie Sie neue Interessen und Aktivitäten entdecken können, die Ihnen Freude bereiten.

Dieses Buch ist nicht nur eine Anleitung, sondern auch eine Begleitung auf Ihrem Weg zur Heilung. Es bietet Ihnen:

* Eine klare und einfache Anleitung, um Ihren Herzschmerz zu überwinden

* Praktische Übungen und Fragen, um Ihre Gefühle zu reflektieren und Ihre Fortschritte zu überwachen

* Eine unterstützende und motivierende Atmosphäre, um Sie auf Ihrem Weg zu begleiten

Wenn Sie bereit sind, Ihren Herzschmerz zu überwinden und ein neues Leben zu beginnen, dann ist dieses Buch genau das Richtige für Sie. Es ist ein Buch, das Ihnen hilft, Ihre Gefühle zu verarbeiten, Ihre Stärken zu entdecken und Ihren Weg zur Heilung zu finden.

Zielgruppe

* Menschen, die unter Herzschmerz leiden

* Menschen, die eine Trennung oder einen Verlust erlebt haben

* Menschen, die sich allein oder hilflos fühlen

* Menschen, die nach einer Anleitung suchen, um ihren Herzschmerz zu überwinden

American Shadows: Hecate's Intervention - The Unofficial Sequel to American Gods

Embark on an electrifying journey in this unofficial sequel to Neil Gaiman's "American Gods" that will keep you on the edge of your seat!

Shadow Moon's world is turned upside down once again as he grapples with his demigod heritage and the betrayal of his father, Odin. As deities from pantheons across the globe and modern incarnations clash in a high-stakes game of power, Shadow must navigate a treacherous landscape of alliances, deceptions, and hidden agendas.

Key characters return with a vengeance:

Shadow Moon - wrestling with his newfound powers and uncertain destiny

Laura Moon - resurrected and seeking retribution against the gods who manipulated her

Odin - plotting from the shadows, gathering old allies for a mysterious purpose

Bilquis - forging an unexpected alliance that could reshape the divine order

Loki - weaving elaborate schemes to manipulate gods from various mythologies

New threats emerge as Hecate, the Greek goddess of magic and crossroads, stirs up chaos faster than anyone anticipated. With the boundaries between realms blurring, Shadow must confront his past, forge unlikely alliances, and unlock the full potential of his divine lineage.

"American Shadows" delivers a masterful blend of global mythology, suspense, and character drama that will captivate fans of the original and newcomers alike. Prepare for a rollercoaster ride through a world where gods from every corner of the earth walk among us, technology births new deities, and the fate of multiple realms hangs in the balance.

Will Shadow embrace his destiny or fall victim to the machinations of gods both ancient and modern? The answers lie within these pages, where every shadow conceals a secret and every choice shapes the fate of worlds.

Step into the shadows – your journey through a rich mosaic of global mythologies continues here!

Kosmische Matrix: Heilige Geometrie zum Ausmalen

"Kosmische Matrix" opens the fascinating world of sacred geometry. This coloring book serves as a meditative journey through universal patterns, inviting creativity and reflection. Perfect for enthusiasts of sacred geometry and those seeking a relaxing yet profound creative break, each page offers timeless designs to bring to life with color.

Herzklopfen für die Ewigkeit: Der Weg zu dauerhafter Liebe

Entdecken Sie den Schlüssel zu einer erfüllten, dauerhaften Partnerschaft!

In "Herzklopfen für die Ewigkeit" nimmt Sie Psychotherapeut und Autor Dirk Werner mit auf eine faszinierende Reise durch die Wissenschaft der Liebe. Erfahren Sie, wie biochemische Prozesse und neuronale Verbindungen unsere Gefühle beeinflussen und wie Sie dieses Wissen nutzen können, um Ihre Beziehung zu vertiefen. Erkunden Sie die Welt des bewussten und unterbewussten Denkens und entdecken Sie, wie diese Prozesse Ihre Partnerschaft prägen und stärken können.

Dieses Buch bietet Ihnen:

- Einblicke in die Neurobiologie der Liebe
- Verständnis für die Rolle des Unterbewusstseins in Beziehungen
- Praktische Strategien zur Stärkung emotionaler Bindungen
- Techniken für achtsame Kommunikation und Konfliktlösung
- Methoden zur persönlichen Weiterentwicklung als Beziehungspartner:in

Egal, ob Sie am Anfang einer Beziehung stehen oder Ihre langjährige Partnerschaft neu beleben möchten - "Herzklopfen für die Ewigkeit" gibt Ihnen die Werkzeuge an die Hand, um eine tiefe, erfüllende Verbindung zu schaffen und zu erhalten.

Lassen Sie sich inspirieren und entdecken Sie, wie Sie das anfängliche Herzklopfen in eine lebenslange, liebevolle Bindung verwandeln können. Ihre Reise zu einer dauerhaften Liebe beginnt hier!

The Simulation Chronicles: A Mind-Bending Sci-Fi Thriller Where Reality is the Ultimate Illusion

What if everything you believe is a lie?

Alex Stone, a spiritual guide, reunites with Leo Carter, a man haunted by his past and tormented by unseen forces known as "Negs." These negative entities lurk in the shadows of our simulated reality, feeding on human energy and exploiting our weaknesses. They are drawn to fear, doubt, and trauma, amplifying our darkest emotions and manipulating us for their own sinister purposes.

Their quest for answers reveals a terrifying truth: Earth is not what it seems. It's a simulated reality, the 3rd Dimension in a vast, eleven-dimensional system, and humanity is trapped within its confines, vulnerable to the insidious influence of Negs.

But they are not alone.

Joining forces with Zara, a powerful Mystic, and Kai, a fierce Warrior, they embark on a mind-bending journey across dimensions, battling Negs and confronting the powerful Archons who control the simulation. They must learn to navigate the treacherous landscape of this artificial reality and master unique defenses to fight for the fate of humanity.

Prepare yourself for:

A reality-bending adventure that will challenge your perceptions.

Ancient secrets and powerful forces beyond human comprehension.

The struggle to master unique defenses and fight for the fate of humanity.

Uncover the truth behind the simulation and escape the illusion. Your journey begins with The Simulation Chronicles.

This book is perfect for fans of:

The Matrix

The Celestine Prophecy

Jonathan Strange & Mr. Norrell

Ready Player One

Souverän durch ihre Tests: Ein Handbuch für Männer

Confidently through her tests: A handbook for men

Discover the secrets to mastering the subtle tests - from first encounters to long-term relationships. This practical guide reveals why women test and how to respond authentically and confidently.

What can you expect?

- Insights into psychology: Understand the deeper motivations behind testing

- Early detection: Identify tests on the first date

- Proven strategies: React confidently in every phase of the relationship

- Personal growth: Strengthen your self-confidence and your boundaries

Whether you're single or in a relationship, this book will provide you with valuable insights and practical tips to better understand and navigate interpersonal dynamics.

Start your journey to fulfilling relationships today. Learn how to be authentically present while deepening your connection with your partner.

For men who want to grow in love and relationships - your guide to greater understanding, trust and true intimacy.

Souverän durch ihre Tests: Ein Handbuch für Männer

Entdecken Sie die Geheimnisse, um die subtilen Tests zu meistern – von der ersten Begegnung bis zur langfristigen Beziehung. Dieser praktische Ratgeber verrät, warum Frauen testen und wie Sie authentisch und selbstbewusst reagieren.

Was erwartet Sie?

- Einblicke in die Psychologie: Verstehen Sie die tieferen Beweggründe hinter Tests

- Früherkennung: Identifizieren Sie Tests beim ersten Date

- Bewährte Strategien: Reagieren Sie in jeder Phase der Beziehung selbstbewusst

- Persönliches Wachstum: Stärken Sie Ihr Selbstvertrauen und Ihre Grenzen

Ob Sie Single sind oder in einer Beziehung, dieses Buch bietet Ihnen wertvolle Einblicke und praktische Tipps, um zwischenmenschliche Dynamiken besser zu verstehen und zu steuern.

Beginnen Sie noch heute Ihre Reise zu erfüllenden Beziehungen. Lernen Sie, wie Sie authentisch präsent sein und gleichzeitig Ihre Verbindung zu Ihrem Partner vertiefen können.

Für Männer, die in der Liebe und in Beziehungen wachsen wollen – Ihr Leitfaden für mehr Verständnis, Vertrauen und wahre Intimität.

Verhängnisvolle Trance: Dr. Seelmanns erster Fall

Im Herzen Münchens erschüttert ein brutaler Mord die Stadt. Dr. Lukas Seelmann, ein brillanter Psychologe mit einer besonderen Gabe für Hypnose, wird in die Ermittlungen hineingezogen. Gemeinsam mit der resoluten Hauptkommissarin Jana Wehring taucht er in die Schatten der bayerischen Metropole ein.

Von den eleganten Galerien der Schickeria bis in die düsteren Gassen des Hasenbergls folgen sie einer Spur, die tiefer führt, als sie je ahnten. Seelmann muss seine unorthodoxen Methoden einsetzen und sich seinen eigenen Dämonen stellen, um die Wahrheit ans Licht zu bringen.

Doch je näher sie der Lösung kommen, desto gefährlicher wird es. Ein Netz aus Korruption, alten Geheimnissen und tödlichen Intrigen zieht sich um sie zusammen. Können Seelmann und Wehring den Fall lösen, bevor es zu spät ist?

"Verhängnisvolle Trance" ist der fesselnde Auftakt einer neuen Krimireihe. Lassen Sie sich in einen packenden Thriller ziehen, der Münchens glanzvolle Fassade durchbricht und Sie bis zur letzten Seite in Atem hält.

• Für Fans von Sebastian Fitzek und Michael Tsokos

• Ein atmosphärischer Krimi mit psychologischer Tiefe

• Perfekt für Leser, die komplexe Charaktere und unerwartete Wendungen lieben

Entdecken Sie Dr. Seelmanns ersten Fall und lassen Sie sich von der verhängnisvollen Trance mitreißen!

Fatal trance: Dr. Seelmann's First case (Series: Dr. Seelmann's Mysterious Cases – English Edition)

In the heart of Munich, a brutal murder shakes the city. Dr. Lukas Seelmann, a brilliant psychologist with a special gift for hypnosis, is drawn into the investigation. Together with the resolute chief inspector Jana Wehring, he delves into the shadows of the Bavarian metropolis.

From the elegant galleries of the chic crowd to the dark alleys of the Hasenberg, they follow a trail that leads deeper than they ever suspected. Seelmann must use his unorthodox methods and face his own demons to uncover the truth.

But the closer they get to the solution, the more dangerous it becomes. A web of corruption, old secrets and deadly intrigue tightens around them. Can Seelmann and Wehring solve the case before it's too late?

"Verhängnisvolle Trance" is the gripping prelude to a new crime series. Let yourself be drawn into a gripping thriller that breaks through Munich's glamorous façade and keeps you in suspense until the very last page.

- For fans of Sebastian Fitzek and Michael Tsokos

- An atmospheric crime thriller with psychological depth

- Perfect for readers who love complex characters and unexpected twists and turns

Discover Dr. Seelmann's first case and let yourself be carried away by the fatal trance!

Tödliches Echo: Dr. Seelmanns zweiter Fall

Nach den traumatischen Ereignissen seines letzten Falles will sich der forensische Hypnosetherapeut Dr. Lukas Seelmann eigentlich aus den Ermittlungen zurückziehen. Doch als eine Serie makaber inszenierter Morde die Münchner Kunstszene erschüttert, bittet Hauptkommissarin Jana Wehring ihn erneut um Hilfe.

Die Opfer sind bekannte Künstler, ihre Leichen verstörend kunstvoll arrangiert. Die Spur führt Seelmann und Wehring in die geheimnisvolle Welt der Kunsttherapie, wo verdrängte Erinnerungen und dunkle Geheimnisse ans Licht kommen. Als Seelmann tiefer in die Seelen der Verdächtigen blickt, gerät er selbst in den Sog eines tödlichen Spiels, das ihn an die Grenzen seiner Fähigkeiten – und seiner Vergangenheit – bringt.

Doch je näher er der Wahrheit kommt, desto stärker verschwimmen die Grenzen zwischen Kunst und Wahnsinn, Vergangenheit und Gegenwart. Kann Seelmann den Mörder rechtzeitig stoppen, bevor das nächste Opfer fällt?

„Tödliches Echo“ ist ein packender Psychothriller, der die Abgründe der menschlichen Psyche auslotet und mit überraschenden Wendungen bis zur letzten Seite fesselt.

Deadly Echo: Dr. Seelmann's Second Case (English Edition)

After the traumatic events of his last case, forensic hypnotherapist Dr. Lukas Seelmann actually wants to withdraw from the investigation. But when a series of macabre murders shakes Munich's art scene, Chief Inspector Jana Wehring asks him for help again.

The victims are well-known artists, their corpses arranged in a disturbingly artistic manner. The trail leads Seelmann and Wehring into the mysterious world of art therapy, where repressed memories and dark secrets come to light. As Seelmann looks deeper into the souls of the suspects, he himself is drawn into a deadly game that pushes him to the limits of his abilities - and his past.

But the closer he gets to the truth, the more the boundaries between art and madness, past and present become blurred. Can Seelmann stop the murderer in time before the next victim falls?

"Deadly Echo" is a gripping psychological thriller that explores the depths of the human psyche and captivates with surprising twists and turns until the very last page.

The Legacy of the Lodges: Dr. Seelmann's 3rd case

Dr. Seelmann's mysterious cases

Discover the world of "The Legacy of the Lodges", Dr. Lukas Seelmann's third case, a gripping thriller that will draw you under the spell of dark secrets and dangerous conspiracies.

A mysterious murder in an old Munich cemetery, a second crime in an academy of arts, and a trail that leads to a secret order called the "Guardians of Heritage": Dr. Seelmann and Chief Inspector Wehring find themselves caught up in a maelstrom of secret lodge symbols, Nazi-looted art and occult rituals. A mysterious medallion, grotesque works of art and an ancient grimoire gradually reveal a conspiracy that goes back centuries. The line between reality and fiction becomes blurred as they delve deeper and deeper into the dark secrets of the secret society that builds its power on hidden knowledge. Will they uncover the truth before they themselves become victims of an ancient secret society? A suspenseful thriller that will keep you gripped until the very last page!

"The Legacy of the Lodges" is a suspenseful thriller that will keep you gripped until the very last page. A labyrinth of secrets, conspiracies and occult practices awaits you. Are you ready to discover the truth?

Das Vermächtnis der Logen: Dr. Seelmanns dritter Fall

Dr. Seelmanns mysteriöse Fälle

Entdecke die Welt von "Das Vermächtnis der Logen", Dr. Lukas Seelmanns drittem Fall, einem fesselnden Thriller, der dich in den Bann düsterer Geheimnisse und gefährlicher Verschwörungen zieht.

Ein rätselhafter Mord auf einem alten Münchner Friedhof, ein zweites Verbrechen in einer Akademie der Künste, und eine Spur, die zu einem geheimen Orden namens „Wächter des Erbes" führt: Dr. Seelmann und Hauptkommissarin Wehring finden sich in einem Strudel aus geheimen Logensymbolen, NS-Raubkunst und okkulten Ritualen wieder. Ein geheimnisvolles Medaillon, groteske Kunstwerke und ein uraltes Grimoire enthüllen nach und nach eine Verschwörung, die Jahrhunderte zurückreicht. Die Grenze zwischen Realität und Fiktion verschwimmt, als sie immer tiefer in die dunklen Geheimnisse des Geheimbundes vordringen, der seine Macht auf verborgenem Wissen aufbaut. Werden sie die Wahrheit aufdecken, bevor sie selbst Opfer eines alten Geheimbundes werden? Ein spannender Thriller, der Sie bis zur letzten Seite fesseln wird!

"Das Vermächtnis der Logen" ist ein spannungsgeladener Thriller, der dich bis zur letzten Seite fesseln wird. Ein Labyrinth aus Geheimnissen, Verschwörungen und okkulten Praktiken erwartet dich. Bist du bereit, die Wahrheit zu erfahren?

Did you love *How to Recognize Cults: A Guide to Protecting Yourself from Manipulation and Control*? Then you should read *The Battle Within: A Guide to Overcoming Inner Struggles*[1] by Dirk Werner!

[2]

"The Battle Within: A Guide to Overcoming Inner Struggles" is a profound and insightful guide designed to help readers navigate the complex landscape of inner struggles. This eBook delves into the psychological aspects of personal conflicts, offering readers a deep understanding of the forces shaping their internal experiences.In this transformative journey, readers will discover the crucial role of childhood experiences, societal influences, and personal beliefs in forming their current challenges. The book emphasizes the importance of communication and boundary-setting as tools for managing these struggles, providing practical advice and strategies to apply in everyday life.Each chapter is a step towards self-discovery and healing, addressing common emotional battles such as anxiety and depression, and guiding readers towards fostering healthier relationships. This guide is not just about overcoming difficulties; it's

1. https://books2read.com/u/b5Bpxp

2. https://books2read.com/u/b5Bpxp

about empowering individuals to make significant, positive changes in their lives.Whether you're seeking to understand the roots of your inner conflicts or looking for ways to foster your personal growth, "The Battle Within" offers a compassionate, insightful, and practical approach to achieving emotional well-being and self-empowerment.

Read more at https://www.dirk-werner-psychotherapie.de.

Also by Dirk Werner

Dr. Seelmanns mysteriöse Fälle

Verhängnisvolle Trance: Dr. Seelmanns erster Fall
Tödliches Echo: Dr. Seelmanns zweiter Fall
Deadly Echo: Dr. Seelmann's Second Case
Das Vermächtnis der Logen: Dr. Seelmanns dritter Fall
The Legacy of the Lodges: Dr. Seelmanns 3rd case

Psychotherapie: Mittel und Methoden

Gemeinsam den Weg gehen: Empathie im Umgang mit psychischen Erkrankungen für Angehörige und Patienten

Thought Leader

Emotionale Intelligenz und Leadership: Wie Sie Ihre Stärken optimal nutzen

Standalone

Dankbarkeit im Alltag: Ein interaktives Tagebuch für mehr Zufriedenheit und Lebensfreude
The Battle Within: A Guide to Overcoming Inner Struggles
Suizidprävention: Basics
101 goldene Regeln für eine harmonische Paar-Beziehung
Selbstsabotage überwinden: Entfessle dein wahres Potenzial

Self-Love Over Perfection: A Guide to Overcoming Female Narcissism
American Shadows: Hecate's Intervention - The Unofficial Sequel to American Gods
Nanogenesis: The Rise of Superhumans
The Simulation Chronicles
Herzklopfen für die Ewigkeit: Der Weg zu dauerhafter Liebe
How to Recognize Cults: A Guide to Protecting Yourself from Manipulation and Control
How to Recognize Cults: A Guide to Protecting Yourself from Manipulation and Control

Watch for more at https://www.dirk-werner-psychotherapie.de.

About the Author

Dipl.-Psych. Dirk Werner has been working as a psychotherapist for 25 years. As a psychological psychotherapist, he mainly works in his own outpatient psychotherapeutic practice.

www.dirk-werner-psychotherapie.de

https://books2read.com/u/b6lwrA

https://www.xing.com/profile/Dirk_Werner12

https://de.linkedin.com/in/dirk-werner-657a81a8

Read more at https://www.dirk-werner-psychotherapie.de.

www.ingramcontent.com/pod-product-compliance
Lightning Source LLC
LaVergne TN
LVHW090358210926
848480LV00002B/382